INTEGRATED EDUCATION

INTEGRATED EDUCATION

P. Sam Daniel
Rachel K. Daniel

KALPAZ

Integrated Education

ISBN: 978-81-7835-937-7

Published in 2012 in India by
Kalpaz Publications
C-30, Satyawati Nagar,
Delhi - 110052
E-mail: kalpaz@hotmail.com
Ph.: 9212729499

Laser Type Setting: Rajender Vashist, Delhi
Printed at: Chawla Offset Printers, Delhi

Dedicated to

Mrs. RACHEL GNANASIGAMONY

Whose faith and love brought many blessings to three generations to continue her legacy

Contents

Foreword

I

I deem it an honour and privilege to write the foreword to the book entitled Integrated Education authored by Dr. Sam Daniel and Rachel K. Daniel, educationists with vast experience both in India and abroad. Author of many books and scholarly articles, the present work is the masterpiece of Dr. P. Sam Daniel as an experienced educationist. I wish the authors good success and pray that many more books on education may be brought to light by them. I hope that those who are engaged in education may make use of the present work for the better fulfillment of the mission entrusted to them.

In the globalized world Indians have a great role to play in moulding the future destiny of the world. Indian system of education is well-appreciated all over the world and as a result our doctors, engineers and other skilled workers occupy key positions and rendering vital services to the humanity at large. The great challenge before India is to popularise education and make available the benefits of higher education to the millions of people in the remotest villages of India. We are a nation blessed with large number of human resources. The success of India depends on how far the benefits of education cold be made available to the Indians who are marginalized, less privileged or depressed.

Integrated education which encompasses head, heart and hands is very much of the education of India tradition. The beautiful Indian expressions and practices like ‘Samanvaya’, ’Gurukul’ and ‘Samavada’ elegantly articulate and beautifully express the Indian understanding of integrated education. Getting inspiration from traditional Indian thoughts on education, the authors try to evolve a new philosophy of education taking into serious consideration the rapidly changing Indian and world scenario.

Going through the book one gets the impression that the present work is a response to the urgent need for a guideline to evolve an integrated education especially in the context of the fragmented formatting of our younger generation. The beauty and uniqueness of this book lie in the fct that there is a healthy synthesis and blending of the Eastern Western and Indian philosophies of education with a detailed study of the contributions of the eminent people like Gandhi, Tagore, Whitehead and Dewey. The authors also bring to light the current developments in integrated research, issues and challenges in integrated education, which enable the reader or scholar to plan future projects in the field of education.

The authors through the 11 chapters present in a comprehensive way the points to be discussed while dealing with the topic integrated education. In a world where education is being commercialized, where survival of the fittest is the order of the day, the Integrated Education has something to say in a unique way especially through the chapter on Ethics and

Values in Integrated Education. True education imparts values which include respect for others and respect for the nature, which eventually leads to a new world order, a new humanism, where caste, colour creed, social status, etc. have no role to play in relating oneself to another, where corruption has no place, where individuals are judged on the basis of merit, not on the basis of favouralism, where the joys and sorrows of one's neighbour is one's own joys and sorrows. May the integrated education help us to transform the society.

I wish and pray that the efforts of the authors bear abundant fruits and the present work inspire all those who are directly or indirectly involved at different stages of education and in the formation of the future generation.

Francis Thonippara, CMI
President, DVK

II

As an experienced secondary teacher and now tertiary teacher educator in large prestigious western university, I am well aware of the impact that the huge societal changes of the 21st century have had on both learning and teaching. It was therefore a pleasure to read the insightful guidance provided in the book *Integrated Education* by Sam and Rachel Daniel. Integration is discussed not jst in terms of curriculum or content, but as an entire approach to teaching and learning, something which has been notable in its absence from much of the current body of literature dealing with this important topic.

Integrated Education is a timely publication. It has been written for a period where education systems around the globe are struggling to provide for a student cohort that is very different from previous generations. Technology plays a much larger role in our Education systems today, but this also paves the way for depersonalization and the concomitant de-emphasis of relationships. However, as is so aptly pointed out in this book – education must be all encompassing it it is to meet the needs of our changing society, where issues of globalization, technology and diversity are relatively new challenges. The authors argue that the head, the heart and the hands must all be involved which i9s a much nicer way of stating that we need a true integration of the cognitive, the affective and the physical at every stage of the education process.

The authors have managed to capture the essence of integration through coverage of its many layers but I was particularly impressed with the focus on ethics an values as this is one area which I believe needs to be prioritized. With the ability to gain access to large bodies of information in very short time frames, there needs to be equivalent emphasis on the moral and ethical implications for this in how we learn and teach.

I found the chapters outlining the range of 'educators' who have obviously influenced the vision of the authors, particularly enlightening. These chapters provide a valuable reference point for where the authors are situated both philosophically and educationally. To see the integration of the Eastern and

Western influences was another example of how the authors have practiced what they preach in terms of true integration. A further example is the inclusion of a practical model for integration, illustrating how they have attempted to integrate theory and practice.

Overall, I believe that Integrated Education is a valuable and timely resource for educators who wish to focus on a more holistic approach to learning and teaching. It is important to remember – that becoming educated involves more than just knowing – it is about thinking, feeling and doing and I think this book provides important guidelines for how this light be accomplished.

As an educator for the 21st century, I commend this book to you.

Dr. Margaret Plunkett
Coordinator and Senior Lecturer
Faculty of Education
Monash University, Australia
http://www.education.monash.edu.au/profiles/plunkett

Preface

Integrated Education impacts not just the mind but encompasses a person as a whole, that is, head, heart and hands. It will help students to integrate them into society and to bring out social change as per the needs of the global environment. It will also integrate the modern Information Communication Technologies for the overall development of the education system. Education ideals and philosophies of the past and present, the East and the West will make the education process for total development and will help to make one a complete man. The traditional teacher centred education system will be changed to student centred one providing ample opportunities for the students to involve in the entire process and to encourage them to be creative. Integrated Education will integrate the teacher and the taught to make the teaching-learning process relevant to real life situation. The concept of academic-industry interaction will integrate students to develop their skills and potentials to the maximum.

In the era of global connectedness and competition, it is inevitable to have international comparisons. The learning outcomes across the world are distorted according to what is taught and how it is taught. In an integrated atmosphere, students need to have understanding in and across the major disciplines, that is, scientific understanding, historical understanding, artistic/humanistic understanding and mathematical understanding. This is best done by providing new opportunities for the student to explicate. It is also necessary to make students to become moral and ethical citizens.

Challenges faced by traditional education in the light of the disruptive potentials of the new digital media is another development in the educational scenario. Parents, the community, religion, service organisations and media should participate in the education process, and to preserve the ancient but still important values. An integrated course should be more flexible, creative in its style of teaching and learning, on the one hand, and the struggle to do well on a single test instrument which valorises having lots of information and being able to give it back on demand on the other. One of the challenges is to watch the students and to see what interests them, and find ways to help them follow that talent or passion. This does not mean ignoring what is important in school, but it does mean realising that life is more than school and that finding one's passion can make the difference.

Regarding the issues on mother tongue education versus English medium education, it may depend on the region, the religion, the family options and dynamics. The decisions about language need to be made in terms of what is in the best interest of the child in the long run. Uniform system of education is another matter for concern. There are vast differences in resources utilised for education. Individual learners are not all the same and they should not be treated as if they are. To provide quality education for every child and spending more resources for disadvantaged children are considered the best education systems in the world.

Chapter 1 on "Introduction to Integrated Education", introduces the subject, "Integrated Education" in a precise way. Integrated Education will lead one to reach ones head, heart and hand. Through Integrated Education we can bring together the best of our education system with the modern technological development and enhance a holistic development of a person into a complete man. There should be a positive interaction between the student and the teacher that encourages creativity. Eastern and Western education systems of the past were centred around everyday life of individuals and society. There was much real life connection in the teachings of major philosophical, cultural, religions traditions of Hinduism, Buddhism, Christianity, Islam and Confucianism to integrate education to impact culture and society. The concepts on Integrated Education, Integrated Curriculum, Integrating Technology into the Pedagogical Process,

Globalisation of Higher Education, Work Integrated Studies are introduced in this chapter.

Chapter 2 deals with "Globalisation and Integrated Education". Globalisation is a process of promoting and enhancing interconnectedness among individuals, groups, institutions, companies and countries brought about by technological, economic and political changes. Academic globalisation has made the Indian Universities players in international market. Application of university governance embraces all sectors from curriculum, examination, research and development activities, ensuring adequate human and physical facilities to optimal resource allocation through evolution of the modern concepts of employee empowerment. Impact of globalisation on education has brought out online education courses, availability of educational job option globally, call for redefining, rearranging, adding and improving the aims and objectives of education. Integrated education in this context will help to explore new horizons and transform the present narrowly conceived education into a multifaceted comprehensive, integrated programme of real value addition in several domains of students overall development.

Chapter 3 on "ICTs in Integrated Education" brings out the importance/role of ICTs as a potential power and enabling tool for educational change and reform. The effective integration of ICTs into the educational system is a complex, multifaceted process. ICT education can be classified into four main categories in integrated higher education, such as, e-learning, U-learning, Blend learning and Distance learning. Effectiveness, cast, equity and sustainability are four intertwined issues which must be addressed when considering the overall impact of the use of ICTs in Integrated education. ICT supported learning encourages interaction and cooperation among students, teachers and experts regardless of where they are by integrating them in the educational process in a meaningful way.

Chapter 4 is on "Ethics and Values in Integrated Education" Value additions on Integrated Education propounded by eminent philosophers and thinkers are presented in this chapter. Inculcating and creating the right environment will help and encourage young minds to resolve personal and moral issues independently are of utmost importance. Modern education had adversely changed with the main objective of passing the examinations with good marks, but has ignored the heart. Education today is teaching the youth to live by machines and gadgets and not by universal human values like truth, non-violence, love and compassion. Integrated Education advocates to instill in the youth awareness and respect for values and ethics and commitment to their culture, peace and understanding, justice and fairplay, rule of law with spiritual hunger for the higher goals. The role of education is to culture the individual in such a manner that he himself lives blissfully and also contributes to the society in its progress and peace.

Chapter 5 on "Curriculum for Integrated Education" gives some concrete suggestions for developing curriculum for Integrated Education. In an integrated approach the curriculum of a programme cuts across subject matter lines. It underscores learning and teaching in a holistic way. Curriculum is not just a series of jumbled subjects but a permutation of subjects intertwined, interactive and collaborating with one another. It depends upon what, which and whom it is meant for. Activity oriented and learner centred curriculum, could provide scope for application dimension as well as for multi-skill and holistic development, along with an emphasis on value oriented and social outlook.

Chapter 6 on "Gandhi on Integrated Education" has given an account of Gandhi's Philosophy and pragmatic approach to Integrated Education. Education formed an important competent of his writings for more than half a century. Gandhian philosophy was based on the supreme value of 'Truth'. Education for him was not an endeavour for lifelong process. It also included the nationalistic goals. Education is for the body, mind, life and soul. Ethics he considered the foundation of education. He reiterated the fundamental principle of national education that each nation has to evolve its own educational ideal based on its cultural heritage, needs and aspirations. His support for co-education, sex education and recognition of place of English in higher education, universal basic education and opposition to corporal punishment are all part of modern systems of education.

Chapter 7 on "Tagore on Integrated Education" explores

the greatness of Tagore and his contribution to education, in particular. His ideal of education is consistent with his ideals of life. The highest mission of education is to help us realise the inner principle of unity of knowledge and all the activities of our social and spiritual being. Tagore's version on education was deeply routed in one's immediate surroundings but connected to the cultures of the wider world. He insisted on pleasurable learning and individualise to the personality of the child. He emphasised on the use of mother tongue as the medium of instruction. His philosophy of education also mentions that equal free educational opportunities for all. Curriculum should orbit organically around nature. Tagore's educational theories evolved out of an attempt to grapple with issues first on an individual, then on a local and finally on an international basis. Tagore showed the way to integrated education for the formation of a complete man.

Chapter 8 on "Whitehead on Integrated Education", is the expression of the West on education in the 20th Century. His process of philosophy posits a view of the world as a developing web of inter connection rather than disjointed parts of or a static monolith. For Whitehead, the principal enemy in the classroom was inert ideas static, irrelevant notions that move neither the hearts nor minds of students. Whitehead's thought on education emphasises process and engagement within a changing world. An integrated system will find itself adjusting to these changes and interpreting unchanging truths in the instability of our times. His philosophy of education was built on the concepts of the organism and process of thought. He always believed that application of the relation of the whole to the part was central to understanding reality. All things depend upon each other. Students do not present their isolated minds or bodies but themselves as integrated human beings whose relations in the world are experiences. The idea of integrated education is based on Whiteheads philosophy of organism. It urges us to turn from reductionism and instead, to think of the whole in relation to the parts and parts in relation to the whole. Integrated Education is to integrate the different parts of a human being for making a whole person, to integrate the different cultures for creating a culture with global view, to develop the student's creativity so that they can translate the knowledge into real wisdom.

Chapter 9 on "John Dewey on Integrated Education", deals with Dewey as an educational thinker. Dewey's theory of knowledge is based on the organic evolution of man's mind that includes aspects of thinking, feeling and willing. The primary activity is in the instinctive, impulsive attitude and activities of the child but these powers of habits and interests get activated against the social background. For him education is reorganisation and reconstruction of experience. Dewey's views continue to strongly influence the design of educational approaches such as in outdoor education, adult training, experimental therapies and various other innovations in learning environments. He was also critical of a completely free, student-driven educational system believing that students needed to structure their own learning experiences for maximum benefit. Dewey argues that educative experiences could be judged by whether or not the individual grow, or would grow, intellectually and morally, the larger community, benefited from learning over the long haul. Dewey advocates for a way of teaching and learning one where students are active in their learning and where experiences make sense to them and are useful.

Chapter 10 on "Current Developments in Integrated Research" analyses the recent developments in the field of research which will have direct impact on Integrated Education. In the development of knowledge two things are happening simultaneously, one micro specialisation, the other integration and inter relationship between different disciplines. Knowledge is developing most rapidly at the intersection of disciplines. Integration takes us away from too much specialisation that many a times prove to be ineffective. Three new methods are introduced here, namely, Design-Based Research Method, Creative Approaches to Research and Work Integrated Research. Design Based Research in a systematic but flexible methodology aimed to improve educational practices through integrative analysis, design, development and implementation, based on collaboration among researchers and practitioners in real world settings and leading to contextually sensitive design, principles and theories. Creative Approach to Research is a cross-disciplinary approach in research that reflects the convergence that is now occurring in the fields between epistemology and technology. Work Integrated Research is gaining a greater profile nowadays. Capabilities that are intended to be more integrated and holisitic can be identified and studied in a given field of study using this method.

Chapter 11 on "Issues and Challenges in Integrated Education" will be an eye opener for new perspectives in Integrated Education. Philosophies and Ideals of the past and the present are integrated to bring out better benefits. Early eastern educational methods tended to emerge from everyday life. There were real connections between what has learnt and the lives that were lived. Although these systems were based primarily on religion, they were less fragmented and hence more integrated and related to real life. Integrated education calls to question the traditional gulfs between teacher and learner, and rejects the divisions between physiology, cognation and emotion in the learning process. Furthermore, it embraces the links, rather than the divisions, between the academic discipline (such as, arts and science) and between various subjective and objective epistemologies and methods of inquiry. The urgent need today is to look at holistic, interconnected, and non fragmented models that are integrated into real life are to be recognised. The learning value is maximum as students with the minimum effort make connections among different subject areas and answer various questions as they apply their learning to real life situation. The teacher's role is no longer to control learning but to facilitate it. Community learning has to be integrated. Communities are extensions of individuals, and individuals are extensions of their inner identities and all these need to be integrated to make a dynamic learning process. Another development in Integrated Education is to strike a proper balance between didactic training (knowing from reading and studying) and skills (broadly the ability to do things well), a major departure from essentially 'learning' centric education at present. The future roadmap for Integrated Education needs to include blended methodology, life long learning, collaborative efforts in curriculum development and research, introduction of transnational agencies and increased student mobility.

Acknowledgements

Even though the concept of Integrated Education seems new, we find evidence for such a system being practiced by the philosophers of the East as well as the West from time immemorial. But for quiet a long time Indian Education System has deviated to follow the traditional system of education. In the fast changing world of today, in order to compete we should also make necessary changes in our present education system. One of the authors as a Teaching Associate, Faculty of Education, Monash University, Australia received the necessary exposure to explore further into the Integrated Education System. We thank the University for imparting knowledge on the current developments in Integrated Education. Dr. Ken Gnanakan who was advocating for the development of Integrated learning made a significant impact. Our gratitude to Dr. Aroma G Sam, Mr. John D Kesari and Rev. G. James for the editorial work. Mrs. Vimala Rajagopalan and Mr. P. David Isravel deserve our appreciation for their involvement while finalising the draft. The final responsibility of the work and its judgement about the contents and any errors rest with the authors.

P. Sam Daniel
Rachel K Daniel

1

Introduction to Integrated Education

Integrated Education

The concept of Integrated Education was well conceived in the eastern world encompassing of Integrated Learning, Integrated Teaching, Integrated Curriculum and Work Integrated Learning. Early eastern education system was centred around everyday life. There was interconnection between the learnt and the lives that were lived. Traditions were preserved, religious practices were observed, children were taught values and ethics, and community life was encouraged. There was much real life connection in the teachings of major philosophical, cultural, religious traditions of Hinduism, Buddhism, Christianity, Islam and Confucianism. Buddha, Christ, Mohamed and Confucious proved to be master teachers whose words and deeds brought change world over. In the recent past the teachings of Tagore and Gandhi in the East, and Dewey, Whitehead, Freire and others in the West regenerated and strongly advocated the integrated system of education. The forerunner being Plato in the West.

Integrated Education has to influence not just the mind but to impact the person as a whole. Our education systems today have many positive aspects for development and change; yet it has not touched our heart and mind. Integrated Education will lead one to reach ones head, heart and hand. Education that leads to an vocation is not the end; it has to integrate the person to have an impact on the society that leads to social change. Through integrated education we can bring together the best of our education system with modern technological development and enhance a holistic development of the person into a complete man. Education system that is static has been carried out for generations. Teacher – centred education system will have only limited objectives, where students direct involvement will be curtailed, thereby, resisting change. Creativity in the classroom is either shifted or completely lacking. There should be positive interaction between students and teachers that encourages creativity.

Integrated Learning

Confucius stated, "Tell me, and I will forget, show me, and I may remember. Involve me, and I will understand." World over higher education is passing through an interesting phase. It is changing radically by becoming organically flexible in diversity of programmes, in its structure, in its curricula, in its delivery system and moreover it is adopting itself to the clever use of information and communication technologies. An essential part of this process is the recognition of inevitability of the teaching-learning and evaluation of integrated syllabi. Curriculum is the point of contact between the intentions, which initiate education reforms, and reality of teaching - learning encounters, which ultimately determines the success of changes attempted" (Srivastav and Srivastava, 2003).

For Whitehead, 'Integration' means putting different cultures together, based on positive moral concepts. Every part of the individual-mind, body, emotion and spirit, should be developed at the same time, and be integrated into the whole person. 'Relatedness' is fundamental; nothing is in isolation. 'Everything in this world is in some way connected with every other thing in this world'. Global society needs global education that should be based on the concept of integrated education. According to him, integrated education would be planned to integrate the different parts of human being for making a whole person, to integrate the different cultures for creating a culture with global view, to develop the students activity so that they can translate their knowledge into real wisdom". (Whitehead, 1967) Scholars like whitehead have been calling for changes in our educational system over the decades.

Dewey's Philosophy

John Dewey was influential in bringing significant changes. Dewey's pragmatism has been variously termed as experimentalism, functionalism, instrumentalism, operationalism, parcticalism and progressivism. All these terms indicate the dynamic, ever-changing and performing character of life. Dewey suggested the application of experimental logic. He emphasised that as all experiences cannot be education, the business of the educator is to select an experience or experiences which would enable the individuals to live creatively, constructively, dynamically and faithfully in the changing environment.

Dewey accorded a central place in occupations and other subjects were treated incidentally as ancillary to practical activities. Dewey observed that the students think out how to make cloth, and re-invent the carding frame, tool for spinning and understand the loom. They learn at the same time enough art and science. "Make the construction adequate, make it full, free and flexible, give it a social motive, something to tell and you have a work of art." Likewise, the knowledge of various subjects revolves round such occupations. (Aggarwal, 2005) This is the kind of integration with actual needs around us rather than mere theoretical studies.

Integrated Study

A basic definition of integrated study is one in which learners broadly explore knowledge in various subjects related to a particular subject. For instance, one may be learning geography, but there could be some mathematics, biology, language, etc. Skills and knowledge are developed and integrated into more than one area of study. In keeping with this, a definition of an integrated course is as follows:

An integrated course is one that is organised in such a way that it cuts across subject matter lines, bringing together various aspects of the particular subject in an interaction with other areas of study in order to achieve stated objectives and outcomes of the programme. It views learning and teaching in a holistic way and reflects on issues in the real world making courses meaningful within their particular as well as wider contexts. The curriculum should indicate the kind of knowledge, understanding, interests, values and attitudes that should be developed in the learner.

Interdisciplinary Integration

A modern approach to education demands that the teacher not merely cause the student to learn and memorise new material, but motivate him/her to learn both eagerly and independently. This is not possible until he/she sees the relevancy of any given knowledge for his/her future life. Having to learn new knowledge usually increases tension in the life of the student, which intern influences the quality of his/her learning. Interdisciplinary integration in teaching reduces the amount of time students spend on homework (thus reducing some of the tension), but most importantly, allows the student to view the world holistically. He/she begins to see the place and importance of the new knowledge he/she required to learn. (Education Towards Wisdom, 2006)

Dunu Roy has said that who have learnt through our system of education, were more suited to the needs of the USA. He pointed out that earlier the IITs had a more integrated approach and also taught humanities, ethics and logic. But these subjects were excluded in order to hasten the production of what he called "unreal" technologists. (Outlook, 2007)

Work Integrated Studies

There is always a work study bond that breaks the dichotomy between the 'elite' and workers work oriented education that provides scope for integrating knowledge with ramification of other subjects. It provided the basis for the development of knowledge, skills and attitudes useful for later participation in productive work. It should cover production, maintenance and the technological processes, as well as human relations, organisation management and marketing. Work integration should begin with simple, creative, self-expressional activities performed with locally available material and simple tools. Then, the use of tools should be introduced in a scientific manner. The curriculum should indicate the kind of knowledge, understanding, interests, values and attitudes that should be developed in the learner. (Nambiar, 2007)

Higher Education

We are facing unprecedented challenges in higher education today. "Twenty first century will be the century of knowledge" and that "the social transformation will primarily be centred on education". Now, the utilitarian approach to education is considered, essential for transition form the higher industrial/ post-industrial society to the 21st century "knowledge Society" centred on the fast – developing information and communication technologies. Essentially the transition from the industrial/ post-industrial society to the "knowledge Society" is, in a sense, a transition from the modern western civilisation, (that remained predominant in the latter part of the second millennium) to the global civilisation of the third millennium that would be based on not merely new technologies but also new post-modernist ideologies of the enlightenment era. (Ahluwalia, 2001)

India was changing, the people were realising their potentials and their demands and expectations were rising. But what was lacking was a serious attempt to alleviate the lot of the poor. India must find credible answers to the problem of educating its masses, improving healthcare facilities to them and tackling the menace of corruption. Citing figures, the total number of Indians having higher education was a mere 7 percent compared to 50 percent in the United Kingdom and 47 percent in G-8 countries. Without education and healthcare facilities, there is little chance of productivity going up. (Educate Masses, 2007). While there are increasing educational opportunities for the already educated, if our education is to be integrated into our context these are the areas we must consider. Higher education must be made affordable and available to help develop the underprivileged and the poor by providing scholarships, quota and other incentives.

Further, higher education must not lose sight of values. Meaningful education should stimulate all aspects of human intellectual potentials. One should not simply emphasise on needs of responsible and the authority of knowledge, science, technology and management, but one should also uphold the values supported by the time honoured and potentially valuable disciplines of humanity. It is true that there is explosion of knowledge, but we should not forget there is an erosion of values. There is no replacement for essence of values. It is essential that the students acquire knowledge and understanding of the facts with a sense of respect to the values. One must be morally good otherwise specialised knowledge will resemble as a well trained dog than a harmoniously developed man. (Vinayagam, 2007)

Globalisation of Higher Education

The fast track of globalisation has boosted the increase of transnational higher education during recent years. New providers, delivery methods and programmes have come into the space of internationalisation of higher education :

- The area of values and ethics is one of the serious concerns that this new development is posing.
- India has got the third largest higher education system in the world next to USA and China.
- Two trends that characterise this expansion:

One is the growing imperative of higher education institutions to internationalise to integrate an international/ intercultural dimension into teaching, research and community service in order to enhance their academic excellence and the relevance of their contribution to societies. Higher education institutions have long experience in this area and are rapidly expanding their cooperation with their counterparts around the world. The second trend is the growth of market driven activities, fueled by increased demand for higher education worldwide, declining public funding in many national contexts, the diversification of higher education providers and new methods of delivery. (IAU, 2005)

The new form of globalisation in higher education has exploited the potential of new information and communication technologies to develop new approaches. As a result, the purpose of higher education has been transformed. Universities are no longer exclusively engaged in refinement, preservation and transmission of authorised knowledge, organised within disciplines and the initiation of young people, generally from privileged social backgrounds into a settled intellectual culture. Traditional disciplines have been undermined by epistemological doubts, reductionist imperatives, skills, knowledge redefined in terms of their social and vocational relevance.

Among various levels of education, higher education has pervasive and influential impact on development of nation. Higher education empowers the individual with necessary skills and competence for achieving personal and social goals, which in turn contribute to the development of nation. A recent study of World Bank also supports this view. (Kale, 2006)

According to the report, "Higher Education in Developing Countries: Peril and Promise, published in 2000, presented a powerful message:

> "Higher Education is no longer a luxury; it is essential for survival".

The globalisation phenomenon, which transformed world trade in the latter part of the 20th century is having a profound impact on education at the start of the 21st century. Technology is going to remain the keystone of the century. Innovative forms of education, computer, communication technologies and internet have accelerated the process of education making it viable for the students to study and learn outside their country.

Today no nation can remain in isolation from the rest of the world because it has shrunk into the form of a "Global Village". Higher education is now being considered as a commodity to be bought and sold. Ministry of Human Resource Development is in favour of internationalisation of higher education due to our present need and being a member of the World Trade Organisation. Our former President Abdul Kalam (2007) has rightly said, "A developed India by 2020, or even earlier is not a dream. It need not even be a mere vision in the mind of many Indians. It is a mission we can all take up."

Vision for Integrated Action

We have the mission of transforming India into a developed nation. For this we have identified five areas where India has core competence, for integrated action:

(a) Agriculture and food processing

(b) Education and health

(c) Information and Communication Technology

(d) Reliable and quality electric power, surface transport and infrastructure

(e) Self reliance in critical technologies. These five areas closely interrelated will lead to food security, economic security and national security.

Development Process for Education

Education leads to formation of human capital and is an important investment for the development process. To meet the challenges, four pillars of education were advised by the Planning Commission in 2002. They are:

(a) Learning to know or capacity to absorb new knowledge, whether the young persons mind are being trained so that throughout their lives they can continue to absorb the exploding knowledge that doubles every five years.

(b) Learning to do mean that the knowledge imparted to young people should also make them capable of gainful employment, so that they become productive members of society.

(c) Learning to live together, that is, education does needs to encompass the necessity for young people to become positive and integrated elements of their respective societies.

(d) Learning to be, that is., education must contribute to the all round development of each individual mind and body, intelligence, sensibility, aesthetic sense, personal responsibility and spiritual values. The holistic education must acknowledge the multiple dimensions of the human personality: physical, intellectual, aesthetic, emotional and spiritual thus moving towards the perennial dream of an integrated individual living on the harmonious planet. (Singh, 2003)

These can be achieved by building capacity for research and inquiry, capacity for creativity and innovation, particularly the creative transfer by knowledge, capacity to use high technology, capacity for entrepreneurial leadership and the capacity for moral leadership. Students must learn how to manage knowledge collectively. When the information is networked, the power and utility of information grows as squared as predicted by Metcalfe's law. Information that is static does not grow. In the new digital economy, information that is circulated creates innovation and contributes to national wealth. (Dutta, 2007)

"Any University is judged by the level and extent of the research work it accomplishes. This sets in a regenerative cycle of excellence. Experience of research leads to quality teaching, and quality teaching imparted to the young in turn enriches the research. Research brings transformation and development and also enhances the quality of education. Both research and teachings go together." (Abdul Kalam, 2007)

World Knowledge Platform

"World Knowledge Platform" will integrate the core competencies of the partner countries to develop knowledge products. This platform will enable joint design, development, cost effective production and marketing of the knowledge products in various domains based on the core competence of partner nations in a meeting place for science, technology, industry and management.

"The convergence of Bio, Nano and IT is expected to touch every area of concern to the humanity. The "World Knowledge Platform" will take up the mission, in some of the areas mentioned, which are of utmost urgency to all us in making the world a safe, sustainable, peaceful and prosperous place to live. (Abdul Kalam, 2007)

Contextualising of Higher Education

In the knowledge economy of tomorrow, the learning organisations alone will survive. For its abilities to learn, create, codify and utilise knowledge faster than rivals and quicker than the environmental changes will provide tomorrow's corporations a competitive advantage that is eternally sustainable. The explosion in/of knowledge has impacted society and economy to such an extent that they have begun to measure themselves in terms of knowledge. It is discernible in the fact that they use knowledge as an adjective. In this new economy and society only the fittest i.e., who are capable of being 'adoptative', 'adaptative' and 'adept' would survive. In view of these developments, education in general and higher education, in particular, becomes a fitting background to the issues of higher education in India.

The beginning of 21st century has marked separation of knowledge from information. With the new understanding facilitated by science, man began to manipulate and there after dominate over nature. Religion was rejected as a metaphysical phenomenon. Empirical reality was the sole concern of philosophy and science to be followed by rationality, the basis of modernity. The separation of religious, philosophical and scientific spheres did not take place in our country the way it did in Europe. However, the over emphasis on specialisation in various disciplines led to a reaction against it in the second half of the preceding century in particular when inter-disciplinary studies came into vogue.

Industrial Revolution that has yielded way to information revolution has brought paradigm shift in the scenario. One who has knowledge or access to information, site of information, e.g., Internet, e-libraries, web-sites with an ability to 'search', 'scroll', and select and thereafter interpreting the data will excel others. Also this paves the way for multimedia and technology in placing the best teacher to the remotest part of the country. This will not be an isolated activity but intermingle with society, work, and even leisure. Moreover, learner would become central again in the entire process of education, as he would become a customer seeking qualitative education, customised for his purpose. Only learners would survive in education in the general sense of the term, 'learners', learning teachers, learning educational institutions and organisations.

In the present situation the concept of University has changed considerably. A University in its traditional concept was supposed to be dedicated to the pursuit of knowledge for the sake of it. This concept lent elitist character to universities. Universities have to give up their elitist character based on values in the course of time, and stress shifted to utilitarian aspect. Service to the society became central. Now the universities have begun to play a new role. Knowledge today is for everybody's sake. In practice, India after a signatory to General Agreement on Trade, Commerce and Services (GATS) in 2005, education has been included among 161 services. It would compel us to be professional, qualitative competitors with other players in the educational market from within and abroad.

Indian higher educational institutions should act aggressively and reverse the existing paradigm of foreign universities by having their franchise or educational fairs for attracting Indian students for their courses from abroad. We should explore the possibilities of offering our courses in foreign countries. A modest but firm beginning can thus be made. The collaboration with foreign universities and their presence should be allowed on the basis of reciprocity at least between universities of equal standing. (Singh, 2007)

Quality of Higher Education

It is difficult to measure the quality of education, as it is a service. Quality is a value, not a monetary concept, it is a multiple concept in higher education. It embrace the quality of input such as students, faculty members, the infrastructure, and the process of education covering learning activities, extra-curricular activities, community development activities and the quality of output, in terms of students and graduates. In higher education, research in various disciplines has increased enormously in the last few decades. It has also taken new directions and identified new areas for investigation and exploration. But the concept of quality is diluted. Unprecedented spurt in research obscured concern for quality and as a consequence of this trend, except in few exceptional cases, the output of work is marked by mediocrity and poor quality. Quality control is thus not only important but also very urgent. (Sharam and Venkateshwaralu, 2007)

The UNESCO Report entitled "Learning the Treasure Within", visualises four functions of the universities:

(a) To prepare students for research and training.

(b) To provide training courses to the changing needs of the society.

(c) To be open to all and to foster life long learning in its broadest sense.

(d) To strive for international cooperation.

Economic growth, social welfare and prosperity of a nation depend on its natural resources and the physical as well as mental capabilities of its citizens. However, the talent of the people is more important than natural resources. A study conducted by the World Bank (1994) in 192 countries found that physical capacity and natural wealth account for only 16% and 20% respectively of the total wealth, whereas human capital accounts for the remainder, i.e., 84%. This clearly shows the strong linkage between the socio economic development and education. Education in general and higher education in particular, play a significant role in bringing desirable human capital development. The development of higher education is correlated with the economic development of the nation.

Internationalisation of Indian Higher Education

An unprecedented explosion of scientific and technological knowledge in current panorama has turned the world into a global village. Change and management of change effectively and efficiently have become the clarion call of the era. In the day of explosion of knowledge, expectation and awareness, the 21st century society is bound to be a knowledge based society. A knowledge society is a globally linked borderless one which will impose on institutions the need for international level accreditation and maintenance of standards of the near future. (Aruchami, 2002) It is intellectual capital, i.e., trained manpower rather than financial and physical capital which gives strength and prosperity to the society. In this context, the world of higher education in the 21st century can truly be a borderless world of knowledge and ideas, which will yield reciprocal benefits for all nations. (Periyasamy and Venkatesh, 2004)

Developing a Quality Culture

There is a need to develop a quality culture in our institutions. This will require mental infrastructure more than physical infrastructure because quality depends upon our sincerity of purposes, our vision and conviction to do our duties. The development of such a culture will depend upon the academic leadership of an institution. The leadership must create an environment, which encourage performance. The transformative leadership capable of translating intentions into actions and actions into quality. A leader who can say that his work is his quality. To quote Mahatma Gandhi, "We must be the change we wish to see in the world".

The Chinese Philosopher Confucius stated that the goal of education was to produce men of quality who combined competence with virtue. Thus quality is "multidimensional", and through higher education it strives to develop human resources of global standards. Perceived thus, quality defines the goals and purposes of education. Quality impacts the content of higher education, its processes, its output or product, as it seeks to develop human resources with required skills, excellent performance and capable of delivering the goods as a unit of the work force.

Today there is a strong feeling that the skills of graduates do not match the needs and expectations of the employment sector. Five top skills identified by employers and required of the quality higher education work force are: (1) time management, (2) ability to work under pressure, (3) accuracy and attention to details, (4) oral communication skills, and (5) managing different tasks at the same time. The UNESCO document of Thematic Debate: The requirements of the World and Work," has added a few more to this list, as flexibility, innovation, creativity, entrepreneurship, versatility and teamwork. These skills today are the parameters by which the quality of higher education is assessed. (Dutta, 2007)

Preparing the New Learners of the 21st Century

The profile of the future learners that will fit into the 21st century, as outlined by Sir Christopher Ball has become highly significant. He envisions the future learners to be a flexible generalist rather than a specialist. The flexible generalists are persons equipped with necessary levels of knowledge, skills and values to adjust readily to multiple career changes and make through their own personal development a significant contribution to the life of the country and the world at large. This notion of adaptable world force in the context of the globalisation of economy and the global job market assumes great importance and provides a challenge to the educational institutions.

Modern workforce need to be of the qualities which the practical application of knowledge, confidence, willingness to learn, the amount of information they are exposed to, their urge to excel in the job, ability to lead, ability to accept individual responsibilities, ability to learn new tasks with fewer instructions and wider perspective of life. These interdisciplinary areas and their related technologies are transforming life, and the culture of society as a whole. The challenge therefore is how effectively and how quickly will there be a move away from traditional university type institutions that establish a range of basic social values, and discipline based and knowledge based basic academic skills to a new type of universities that produce flexible all rounder. Hence, any examination reform should attempt to evaluate the overall achievement of students in terms of skills, both cognitive and general, as well as subject related knowledge. (Dutta, 2007)

Abdul Kalam (2007) has recommended five special capacities that are required to be built in education system for nurturing the students. They are, research and enquiry, creativity and innovation, use of high technology, entrepreneurial ability and moral leadership. If we develop these five capacities in our students, we will produce "Autonomous Learners" a self directed, self controlled, life long learners who will have the capacity to both, respect and at the same time is capable of questioning authority in an appropriate manner.

Quality Enhancement (QE)

QE in higher education is a deliberate process of change that leads to improvement. In academic parlance, two terms are used, namely, "Quality Assessment" and "Quality Assurance". The former refers to the internal and external evaluations used to assess the overall teaching and research performance of the institution. The latter refers to the concerns of different stakeholders regarding the continuous process of adopting various mechanisms and procedures to monitor performance and to take up remedial measures to improve the academic standards and to increase the overall effectiveness of the organisation.

The National Assessment and Accreditation Council (NAAC) strives to play the role of a catalyst in synergising the efforts of all stakeholders, namely, the government. the management, the teacher, the parents and the students. It has always been the effort of NAAC to promote participation of students at all levels, in the teaching – learning process on campus. There is a need to provide quality education to students to enable them to play their role as participants in the provision of quality education according to NAAC. (Tara, 2007)

Integrated Curriculum

To evolve integrated curricula for different disciplines, adequately networking with teaching learning and evaluation strategies, based on available infrastructure and human resource factors, socio economic expectations and international norms are involved. Curriculum is the point of contact between the intentions, which initiate education reforms and reality of teaching learning encounters, which ultimately determines the success of changes attempted. Evaluation of achievements of instructional objective, namely, knowledge comprehension and application specified through curricula is an integral part of teaching learning process. Minimum standard of instruction regulations, interdisciplinary merger of skill based courses are essential for the growth and development of the students.

Example:

1. The discipline of plant science have become more applied, since it is fully integrated with economic and industrial development.
2. In China, Basic Science is revamped through a new modernisation programme of economic development, namely, industry, agriculture sciences, technology and national defence.

Higher education should be responsive to the community, whether, regional or local is under considerable discussion at present times. According to policy frame for the development of education in India, adopted by UGC in 1977, every student be given grounding in four essential areas namely: foundation course, core course, applied course, field activities.

Identification of the Factors for the Curriculum Development

1. **Goals and Objectives:** It should be redefined to bring out clarity and direction to the faculty and students, so as to make effective transaction of the curricular contents in the classrooms.
2. **Grounding the Core Disciplines:** Fundamentals of the subject as the core of the disciplines.
3. **Curricula:** Curriculum should not be static. It must change always as frontiers of knowledge expand with the time.
4. **Social Relevance of the contents:** Following three parameters may be considered: (1) Value frame of reference (including philosophical, cultural and ethical values), (2) Economic development, and (3) Social transformation.
5. **Students Need and Interest:** As assessed through systematic interaction with the students.
6. **Pedagogical Techniques:** Suitable methodology for teaching, laboratory study and evaluation should be identified, considering the nature of the content points of the syllabus.
7. **International Norms:** The content area of the curricula should be developed in accordance with current status of knowledge, development and trends of researches carried out in India and Abroad.
8. **Integrating Technology and Pedagogy:** Technology integration is emerging in the information era – educators, media, IT professionals, policy makers, planners, researchers and administrators have to work and plan together.
9. **Evaluation Procedure:** A blueprint of the evaluation tool should be designed on the basis of instructional objectives, content area and forms of the questions, time allocation and difficulty level.
10. **Field Testing:** Developmental try out of curricular materials should be planned to test the validity and reliability of the curriculum. (Daniel, 2007)

Pedagogical Approaches

Interactive Teaching – Learning

Teacher encourages the learners to raise questions and the questions can be immediately probed or investigated by appropriate experimentation in the laboratory or in a simulated experiment on computer or by literature research in the library or on internet. Results of investigation by learners can be presented and discussed in a group to arrive at learning thereof. There can be many ways of engaging group in an interactive mode of learning, which should help create a culture of critical enquiry, analytical thinking and reasoning.

Encouraging experimentation even in subjects which are not amenable to laboratory experiments, as the experiment can be a real time experiment or even a thought experiment. Designing an experiment is a tremendously creative exercise.

Teaching to generate diverse views: consensus is a loss of opportunity in teaching learning. Teacher must bring out hidden queries and encourage informed debates and discussions. Any singular view is not to be dismissed, but seen as an opportunity for a fresh thinking.

Course Evaluation

Formulation of a query for systematic investigation report on latest researches on the subject, a critical comment on a recent research paper or authoring a research article, can constitute instruments of evaluation in a course. 5 to 10% of weightage in a course evaluation to one or more of the above type of evaluation instruments can be allotted.

Two alternative methods of evaluation can be offered in a course form which a learner can choose:

1. The normal method of evaluation in which there are interim tests, quizzes, assignments, etc., followed by semester ending examination.
2. A research based method where the learner may collect a set of data to support concepts/theories taught in the course, then apply the research methodology and prepare a report on a new experiment relevant to course curriculum of the learner may prepare a full research

proposal for a research project at postgraduate level. (Mandke, 2007)

Integrating Technology into the Pedagogical Process

It has been pointed out that irrespective of the nature of technologies deployed, human monitoring, regular enquiry and the use of data in the teaching and learning are essential (Newton. 2000). The biggest challenge in the effective utilisation of Information Communication Technology (ICT) by teachers and its subsequent use in the classroom situation is the creation and integration of effective processes and systems that enable its utilisation in the context spanning different social and cultural contexts. It needs to be kept in mind that ICT will become an effective tool only if it becomes an effective pedagogical tool. (Babu, 2007)

Open and Distance Learning System Pedagogy

It advocates the learner in decision making process at each and every stage of learning from curriculum development to result declaration. Programme evaluation is very much needed by seeking opinions of course users (Learners and Teachers) about various activities and accept the feasible remarks for making the programme more flexible and acceptable for broader use. This may be a qualitative analysis or a quantitative analysis or a blend of both. Also statistical analysis of performance may give some remarkable information on changes so desired. A third evaluation may be also beneficial for the same. All or any of these four techniques may be blended in order to make a meaningful evaluation of the programme. (Rastogi, 2007).

A Creative Model

Ponnavaikko, Vice Chancellor, Bharathidasan University, Tiruchi has announced on 6th Oct. 2007, that skill-based courses and training will be integrated into the curriculum to the students employable immediately after graduation. The Choice-Base Credit System will be customised for the purpose. The university would consolidate its research activities and to set up centres of excellence in innovative areas such as Life Science, Nanotechnology, High Performance Computing and Geosciences. As in the leading universities across the world a

Lab for innovation would be created with facilities for creative students to make original contribution and inventions. To bring underprivileged students into the ambit of higher education, the university would make an assessment on opening colleges in areas of need. The university would work towards creating internet facilities in villages in association with the National Institute of Technology, Tiruchi, under the aegies of Provision of Urban Amenities in Rural Areas (PUARA), the pet project of the former President Abdul Kalam. (The Hindu, Saturday 6. Oct. 2007)

Recommendations for Innovation and Accountability in Integrated Education

- To promote development of a curriculum framework with specific reference to new or emerging of interdisciplinary fields of knowledge.
- To promote the exercise of choice by students for self development, entrepreneurship, acquisition of skills and pursuit of learning, through the development of a flexible academic framework.
- To promote joint and cross disciplinary programmes between and among the educational institutions.
- To promote synergy for research and development in educational institutions, in collaboration with other research agencies and laboratories.
- To promote coordination between educational institutions and industry towards innovations for mutual benefit and for the well being of society.
- To encourage educational institutions to formulate a code of conduct and management to develop a framework code and to guide in their values and ethics of the changing world in general and to the society in particular.
- To develop measures to relate integrated education and research to the world of work and needs of society.
- To take measures to enhance access and inclusion in integrated education and to remove imbalances in the education system of the country.
- To enhance the "standards" in education and research, certain current requirements can be enjoined.

- Specify the requirements for the award of any degree or diploma in any field of knowledge and specify parameters for equivalence between academic qualifications.
- Specify norms and standards of academic quality for accreditation and bench marking of educational institutions.
- Specify norms and mechanisms for transparent, efficient and accountable governance of educational institutions.
- Specific norms to measure the productivity of research programmes and other innovative measures undertaken.

2

Globalisation and Integrated Education

Globalisation

The globalisation is not a new, but an old age concept which was first introduced by Adam Smith in the year 1776 through the book titled, 'Wealth of Nations'. He argued that a country as a whole would gain by having trade relations with other countries. The word globalisation connotes where all the nations join their hands with each other and create a kind of socio-economic environment to do business or any commercial, cultural and educational activities in which every participant nation should be benefited. (Chand, *et al.* 2007).

Globalisation is a process of promoting and enhancing interconnectedness among individuals, groups, institutions, companies and countries brought about by technological, economic and political changes. Capital, technology, management and information are globalised, i.e., organised across national boundaries. The strategic core activities including innovation, finance and institutional management function on a planetary scale on real time. National institutions work as units at the world level. Two of the main bases of globalisation are information and innovation. They are highly knowledge intensives because knowledge is easily portable, and hence, it lends itself easily to globalisation. Certain knowledge becoming obsolete very fast with accelerating development of Information and Communication Technology (ICT), economic units and institutions are required to become learning organisations.

To use new technology to enhance development, India needs (1) adequate internal and external communication, (2) mass education followed by emphasis on science and technology (3) providing a skilled human resource with managerial capability, (4) Research and Development system that adapt new technology to local needs and (5) an integrated structure of research and training institutions. Parallel to the above, India also need: (1) exploratory skills to explore natural resources, (2) exploitation skills to produce those resources efficiently, (3) negotiating skills to establish fair terms of trade with dominant partners, (4) managerial skills to manage products and services efficiently, (5) conservation skills to conserve resources for sustainable development and finally, (6) moral and ethical skills to achieve a just, equitable and fair society.

The United Nations Development Program (UNDP), Human Development Report (1999), has prescribed the distinctive features of globalisation as: Shrinking Space, Shrinking Time and Disappearing Borders. These features are known to be linking people's lives more profoundly, more intensively and more immediately, than was hitherto the case. Globalisation is the growing interdependence of the people across the globe, just as it is a process of integrating not just the economy but culture, technology and governance. Further, globalisation is opening new and diverse opportunities for millions of people around the world, including India. As India is one of the most potential economics of the world, it has to compete effectively in globalisation. (Reddy and Mythily, 2007)

The globalisation is a complex and multi-faceted phenomenon and for the foreseeable future will continue to be a major trend effecting all spheres and levels of society. The early, often passionate, debates about the relative desirability of globalisation have now given way to the growing recognition that this process is not just reversible but also probably unstoppable. Its pace is fast accelerating with a continuous 'free' flow of information, investment capital, human capital, goods and services between countries. However, while globalisation may now appear inevitable the direction and the form it takes is something India can – and must – work to shape. It is the responsibility of all developed, developing and underdeveloped nations to ensure that globalisation serves human interests and is of benefit to all. In other words what the global community aims at is not 'globalisation per se' but 'globalisation with human face.'

So far, the impact of globalisation has been and continues to be unequal. For certain sections of the world community it has been force of economic growth and social mobility, opening up new opportunities for participation and communication. For too many others, however, globalisation has led to deeper marginalisation and impoverishment, widening disparities both within and between countries. Koichirro Matsurra, Director General, UNESCO observed: "Those who suffered from globalisation are invariably those already struggling with exclusion: the poor, women, ethnic minorities and youth." However, whether we like it or not the reality is that the globalisation has come to stay as a reality and the most important challenge or in other words the only option left is to master the art and acquire the skills for harnessing the processes of globalisation, learn from them and adapt best practices so as to reap the beneficial aspects of globalisation by mitigating its negative effects. Parallel to emergence and spread of globalisation there has occurred fast transformation of societies into 'knowledge societies'. Acknowledging this the 21st century has been described as "Knowledge Century Era". In the words of famous Peter Drucker, "The next soeicty will be a knowledge society in which knowledge will be the resource and knowledge workers will be the dominant work force...... In future there would be two work forces made up of the under fifties and the over 50s." (Sharma, 2008)

Academic Globalisation

Academic globalisation has made the Indian Universities 'players' in international market. In order to reap the opportunities of the transnational education system, the universities throughout the world are developing attitude to be a good player in the highly profitable market through strategic planning, improving the quality of teaching and building research capabilities. The internationalisation in higher education sector had reinforced the need to develop a strong and vibrant higher education system to make the institutions the centre of excellence to be internationally competitive and to improve access and equity in higher education. An inequality-enhancing aspects of the academic globalisation is very strong which contributes to progressive reduction in social opportunities.

Higher education is the pivot element of societal formation, nations building and overall economic development. Application of university governance embraces all sectors from curriculum, examination, research and developmental activities, ensuring adequate human and physical facilities to optimal resource allocation through evolution of the modern concepts of employee empowerment. As a signatory to the WTO Agreement, India is now committed to work within the framework of GATS. It means Indian Higher Education scenario is now exposed to unequal competition with transnational educational providers. An uneven race has already been started to grab the market share of this billion dollar education industry. The result of this trade in service sector, higher education has become service rather than means of human resource development where students are being treated as customers. Higher education is now a commodity which is meant for sale in a market which is very much competitive and profitable at the same point of time. Hence there has been a tremendous inflow of private capital particularly in technical higher education. Due to societal shifts from industrial to information age, the 3C's: computer, communication and control are virtually becoming the driving force.

The impact of globalisation on Higher Education has many dimensions:

(i) There has been a massive flow of student across borders. The report 'Global Students Mobilisation 2025' from Australia based Centre for International Economics predicted that India and China would together generate over half of the global demand for international higher education within next 25 years.

(ii) More and more importance on knowledge society.

(iii) Development of trade agreements enhancing trade in education services.

(iv) Mammoth development in information and communication technology.

(v) The growing importance of the concept like educational marketing followed by commercialisation of the educational services.

(vi) Hybridisation of culture.

(vii) Development of joint degrees and growing comparability of qualifications.

(viii) The changed environment featured by Liberalisation, Privatisation and Globalisation (LPG) calls for deep concern regarding quality, equity, equality and access of higher education.

All these elements has promoted lot of new concepts like corporate universities, newer forms of delivering education like distance education, virtual education, diversification of qualification, concept of life long learning, increasing mobility of students, etc. Globalisation in higher education has also introduced several terms in educational scenario like transnational, cross-border, trans-border and borderless education. (Bhowmik, 2011)

Internationalisation and Globalisation

The two terms viz., Internationalisation and Globalisation are clearly overlapping but they are also quite distinct. Internationalisation of the university/higher education can be seen as a series of policies and decisions within the control of the management of the institution – designing and adopting new curricula, international recruitment of both faculty and students and offering of collaborative programmes and undertaking joint research and development projects. In contrast, globalisation tends to be something beyond and institution's control – the flow of technology, new products and processes, knowledge, people, values and ideas across borders. Knight (2003) makes the distinction thus: "Internationalisation is changing the world of education and globalisation is changing the world of internationalisation." Universities and higher education system are agents of both internationalisation and globalisation.

India and China to compete in the global knowledge economy will increasingly depend on whether they can meet the fast growing demand for high-level skills. This in turn, will hinge on their abilities and capacities of the universities to provide quality education that is adapted to the needs of their society and industry. (CERI, 2008). Emerging global institutions are instruments of change and influence and they produce the intellectual capital required by the worldwide society.

Some of the globalisation indexes or indicators relevant to higher education are:

- Percentage of population that uses internet.
- Percentage of population that speaks English
- Percentage of workers who emigrate
- Percentage of population who are immigrants

The other globalisation indexes relate to extent of volume of trade, exports/imports, GDP and capital flow (FDI, Foreign District Investment).

Adopting Foreign Curricular Models and Structures

Many universities have carried out curricular reforms and innovation in their programmes so that their graduates can face the challenges of a global economy. New institutional structures/centres have also emerged to support such curricular innovations and new teaching-learning approaches catering to the 21st century learners.

Globalisation of education will facilitate the transfer of credits, establish academic equivalence of degrees, accreditation of programmes and will enhance the mobility of highly talented and competent workforce across the countries enabling them to seek global opportunities. Globalisation of higher education in Universities in India and China will also further enhance the image of India and China amongst the developed of nations in the world.

Impact of Globalisation on Educational Objectives

With the effect of globalisation in all the areas of life, like economy, culture, society, religion etc., it is very important not only to understand the requirement of redesigning the objectives/aims of education, but also to set up the environment for the smooth working. Privatisation in education sector came with international institutions, online education courses, availability of educational job option globally, call for redefining, rearranging, adding and improving the aims/objectives of education. Following can be the new objectives of the Indian Education System:

- **The aim of self-learning:** Preparing students for learning from the other sources of information.
- **The aim of team work:** With globalisation, team work will be the most wanted competency in the future.
- **The aim of synthesis:** Students need to adapt the skills of synthesis of knowledge with the increase of information of the world.
- **The aim of linking learning:** Variety of information on the same topics and the ocean of information demands linking learning.
- **The aim of adaptability:** With a boundaryless world, those who will adapt will survive.
- **The aim of uni-culture:** Unchecked cultural inclusion in society will demand uni-culture society in the near future.
- The aim of professionalism the nation who gives importance to professionalism is getting strong economically. This is the necessary requirement. (Vyab, 2009).

Student's option for higher (tertiary) education is no longer constrained by national boundaries. Innovative forms of transnational education, i.e., trade in education under the World Trade Organisation (WTO) agreement, internet-based distance learning, branch campuses and educational 'franchising' have greatly expanded opportunities for students to study and learn outside their country of origin. In addition, there is now increasing global competition for the 'best and brightest' students as more and more countries recognise the economic potential of higher education as a service export sector.

But there are also real opportunities for India to get benefited significantly from the global revolution in higher education. To do so, the country requires major policy reforms in the way Indian universities are structured, funded and regulated. It will also require closer interactions between Indian industries, especially the growing technology based sector and Indian universities. And as a whole, it will require a new globally oriented and entrepreneurial style of leadership. With these ingredients, India has the potential to capture the 'up-side' benefits of globalisation and privatisation of higher education emerging with a stronger, better and more globally competitive education system and greater opportunities for Indian students. The government of India has recognised the dangerous phenomenon of brain drain of Indian students with the globalisation of Indian higher education and belatedly started the process of constituting a Committee for the Promotion of India Education Abroad (COPIEA) Department of Education under the Ministry of Human Resources Development.

Impact of Globalisation on Higher Education

Globalisation has a multidimensional impact on higher education. It has increased the need for reforms in higher education with particular reference to large scale utilisation of Information Communication Technology and more emphasis on its research and development activities. Higher education system, as a service industry, is a part of globalisation under the umbrella of General Agreement on Trade and Services (GATS).

From the positive and instrumental perspective, the implications of globalisation for higher education should include maximising the relevance of education to global development and pooling up the best intellectual resource, support and initiatives from different parts of the world for learning, teaching and research. In the era of globalisation, there are major goals of higher education institutions in case of developing countries:

(a) Making the economy globally competitive by training students for employment and knowledge society.

(b) Promoting social inclusion by enhancing opportunities for a wider section of society to obtain higher education in some form whenever they require it with a focus on science and technology.

(c) Changing social structure in response to the needs of time.

(d) Assisting in the process of economic development, particularly of countryside where vast majority of people live.

(e) Establishing close links with their culture and traditions.

Higher Education Institutions are no longer exclusively engaged in the refinement, preservation and transmission of authorised knowledge, organised within disciplines and the initiation of people, generally form privileged social backgrounds into a settled intellectual culture. Traditional disciplines have been undermined by epistemological doubts and reductionist imperatives and skills and knowledge redefined in terms of their social and vocational relevance.

"The revolution in information technology and communication has rendered education portable, flexible, non-linear and student centric. Globalisation in education refers to integrating an international dimension into teaching, learning and service functions of the institutions." (Pradimp 2004)

No doubt, as have been stated above that globalisation is beneficial for the spread of knowledge, technology and culture, yet, sometimes, "these streams move quickly and sometimes erratically, interrupting and destabilising societal connectedness, creating a seemingly boundaryless world of unlimited options, but it is a world severely constrained by increasing surveillance and regulation, terrorism and war and sever inequalities of wealth". (Best and Kelliner, 2001) Today, no nation of the world can remain in isolation from the rest of the world because the world of today has shrunk into the form of a "Global Village." (Sanyal, 2008)

Prerequisites for Globalisation in Education

Certain prerequisites are a must if globalisation in education is to be truly effective:

(1) Emphasis on Quality of Manpower: In the absence of minimum acceptance standards both in schools and in higher and professional education, India loses out on the quality of her manpower. Scientific manpower implies knowledge, skills and a scientific attitude. Our education system produces graduates with at best knowledge of science, but with neither skills nor a scientific attitude. In such a situation, India and other developing countries face an unequal competition in the global competitive market. The problem of quality manpower is further aggravated by the fact that top experts in India are drained away by international attractions and recognition. If the globalisation process is to work out to the advantage of Indian education, we must have a large number of experts in the various disciplines to fall back upon.

(2) **Cross-Country Accreditation and Recognition:** Globalisation will not bear fruit unless Indian institutions and their degrees are recognised and accredited by other countries. A small country like Malaysia recognises only the Indian IIT degrees and nothing else. Even Sri Lanka has not recognised Indian university degrees. This cross-country accreditation and degree recognition cannot be acquired by individual institutions and universities. It will need adequate diplomatic efforts. The Ministry of External Affairs has to play an active role on the globalisation of Indian education.

(3) **Faculty Positions:** If we open the pages of international journals, we find advertisements for senior positions on a global basis. It is not unusual for major British institutions to be headed by Canadian scholars, or US departments by a scholar from India or the Middle East. Is India ready to open up its senior institutional positions to global competition? Will those appointments be recognised and funded by local and central governments?

(4) **Infrastructure Facilities:** Even though the information super highways provide opportunities for the global transfer of knowledge, the developing countries are not yet properly equipped with the necessary exportable goods (knowledge) and vehicles (technologies) to use them. The outdated telecom facilities, high costs of connections, low levels of technological awareness and bureaucratic interference in using the technology may inhibit countries like India from participating actively in the global provision of distance education programme.

(5) **Selective Approach:** The international collaborative arrangements should be based on national priorities. In defining the rules of competition, the nation concerned should use its privilege of regulation to protect its national interest. This selective approach should strengthen the self-sustainability of institutions in developing countries.

(6) **Value Addition:** The local institutions, as partners in the international collaboration, can play an effective and crucial role only when they are capable of making a value addition to the process. This should be done through the adaptation/localisation of materials and services, the sensitisation of the processes to local cultures, etc. This type of contribution will neutralise the possible dominance of resource rich nations.

(7) **State Intervention:** The nation/state may have to intervene actively to minimise the distortions of the globalisation process. The state should subsidise and support the learners from the weaker sections of society to use the opportunities of globalisation of offering scholarships and incentives.

(8) **Role of International Agencies:** The international agencies can strengthen the competencies of the institutions in the developing countries so that they be enabled to cooperate with institutions in the developed countries on equal terms. International agencies should also develop norms and guidelines for globalisation in education to ensure the elimination of unfair competitive practices. (Vyas, 2009)

Meaning of Globalisation in Higher Education

Globalisation of Higher education means growing interdependence and interconnectedness of the globe through increased movement of students and academics over national boundaries due to lowering of barriers for their movements and better international communication. This process is further strengthened by international agreements that facilitate the movement of professionals between the countries. In this way, university education is being treated as commercial product with dealings in it being governed essentially by market forces and the principles of market place.

In this context of higher education, globalisation is a process of integrating science, education, technology, culture and governance. It is going through following four modes:

(a) Operation of educational institutions on foreign land by granting franchise or agreement/arrangement with the educational institutions of the host countries.

(b) Establishment of campuses/centres of foreign universities in host countries.

(c) Establishment of centres by governments of the countries abroad for promoting education and programme offered by other universities/institutions with multiple objectives to enroll more and more international students.

(d) Operation of virtual campuses by using satellite and information super highway. Utilising cyber space has started for marketing education.

The Enabling Framework and the Role of Higher Education

Globalisation has created a global market place for students and scholars. Most students pay tuition enriching the offer of the host countries and draining their own. Moreover, some 80 percent of students from China and India do not return home. In this sense developing countries are relative losers because they invested more in their education. There were more than 200 thousand high level academic scholars largely from developing countries who work outside their home countries to pursue academic work. The important "pull" factors are better salaries, better working conditions and the opportunities at the innovation centres of the developed world. Important "push" factors are limited academic freedom, academic corruption, low salaries and bad working conditions. However, China, India, Brazil and South Africa are benefiting from remittances, research and teaching collaboration facilitated by ICT.

Another consequence of globalisation is the General Agreements on Trade and Services (GATS) adopted by the World Trade Organisation (WTO) in 1995 which put education as a tradable commodity. This has promoted cross-border higher education having its merits and demerits. Among the merits one can cite improvement in quality due to competition, wider access to higher education in country and abroad, use of ICT for delivery, reduction in knowledge gap, decrease in state's financial burden, enhanced capacity building to face dominant partners, reinforcement of national regulatory framework, innovation through new providers and delivery modes. Among the demerits are: increased cost and tuition fees, emergence of a two-tired system: one for rich and another for poor, risk of government indifference, interest of foreign providers in cheap programme with low infrastructure investments and creating "degree mills" with programme of dubious quality and finally a paradigm shift of higher education from a 'missionary approach' to a 'mercenary' approach. In this consumerist, market friendly society greed and corruption, brutal exploitation of natural resources, discrimination will lead the world to destruction if corrective measures are not adopted through education in morality and ethics. (Saravanavel, 2007).

Collaboration

The Globalisation process emphasises on collaboration. The collaboration may be at institution level or individual level. It may be in any area/aspect of higher education, such as, research, teaching, evaluation, curriculum development, instructional material development, etc. Through collaboration, the collaborating institutes or individuals have an access to all facilities available on both sides. This will go a long way in improving the quality of higher education and expanding the possibilities of doing creative work.

Partnership

With the advent of linkages new synergies can be developed and interaction among people can be fostered with the help of a variety of exchange programme. There is a strong need to encourage greater interaction with foreign universities and enhance inter-university partnership at international level. Coombe (1989) defined partnership as, "the range of formal and informal multilateral and bilateral connections between and among individual governments and institutions, on national, regional and international levels, through a variety of development sectors which influence university and college developments." Partnership is such as academic pursuit performed at an interactive level that can make efficient development sense in the way that it not only has the capacity of improving teaching and learning but is also capable of being flexible, efficient, cost effective and economical.

Mutual Understanding

Mutual understanding promotes globalisation of higher education. Majority of problems at international and national levels are due to lack of mutual understanding. Under globalisation of higher education there will be mobility of both students and teachers. They will have experience in understanding the customs, traditions, cultural variations and social dynamics of each other society. It will provide opportunity to change the views and form positive attitude towards each others culture. They can see that each culture has both positive as well as negative attributes. It may develop a sense of oneness which otherwise may not be developed.

Recognition

One of the hurdles in the area of higher education is equivalence as well as recognition of degrees. It is not only a problem at international level but at national too. Within a country, the universities, at times, do not recognise each other's degree. To sort out this problem, universities in India have formed an association, which is known as Association of Indian Universities (AIU). The recognition of degrees as well as their equivalence is decided by AIU, which is accepted by all member universities. (Malgotra, 2007).

Disadvantages of Globalisation on Higher Education

Altbach (2001) reviewed trends in globalisation that have the potential for negative outcome. He said that trends such as the rise of the internet and globalisation of knowledge have the potential for creating severe problems for academic institutions and systems in smaller or poorer nations. In a world divided into centres and peripheries, the centres grow stronger and more dominant and the peripheries become increasingly marginalised. Inequalities grow more pronounced. There is little leeway for academic systems or individual universities to independently develop in the increasingly competitive and fast moving global higher education seen dominated by the world-class universities in the industrialised countries. The traditional academic centre becomes ever stronger and more dominant mainly in the English speaking countries of the North (the United States and United Kingdom and Canada) and in Australia and in the larger countries of the European Union (Notably Germany and France and to some extent Italy and Spain). The norms, values, languages, scientific innovations and knowledge, products of countries in the centre push out other ideas and practices. Globalisation in higher education creates dramatic inequalities among the world's universities. Apart from this, there will be too much standardisation.

It has been pointed out in many quarters that one of the negative impacts of globalisation marked by free flow of goods and human across the boundaries is the emergence and re-emergence of infectious diseases. It is observed that the rapid increase in the number of people travelling over long distances and in the movement of goods across boundaries and oceans introduce new global security issues such as the spread of diseases and pandemics, epidemics like AIDS, Bird-flu, Swine flu which may cause new and rapidly multiplying global health crises. HIV/AIDS with its inter-generational and borderless nature possess an exceptional challenge to human health and welfare. Developments like these require much more attention on the part of those doing science and technology including the policy makers. In fact, there is high expectation to scientific advances in order to fight diseases such as Malaria, Tuberculoses, Cancer, HIV/AIDS, etc.

Current Realities – India's Position in Today's Global Market place

The quality of education and the perceived value of an overseas degree appear to be the most significant factor influencing student decisions to study outside India. The greatest negative impact of WTO or globalisation of higher education would occur in the developing countries like India. These countries have the greatest need for academic institutions that can relevant to the local needs and participate in strengthening of civil society. Globalisation and privatisation of higher education in India will lead to the creation of three different classes of educated students-those educated in foreign universities, those from costly private domestic institutions and those from economically weaker sections studying in government funded institutions. This will only lead to social tensions. In view of the nature of the globalised higher education, the commodification of Indian higher education is about to have an adverse effect on our culture, the ethos of social welfare and even the quality of Indian higher education system. (Chand *et al.*, 2007)

Globalisation and Integrated Education

Long-term Strategy: The short-term measures are intended to make a breakthrough in the conventional by rigid system offering a narrow exposure only for rote learning. The goal in the globalising context of the 21st century and the challenges of the knowledge age is to explore new horizons and transform the present narrowly conceived higher education into a multi-faceted comprehensive, integrated programme of real value addition in several domains of the students' personality. Some of the suggested design of the strategy needed for the purpose are:

Curriculum Designing: The prescribed curriculum by the university/institution be enriched with details needed to supplement it and by filling in the gaps, by adding practicum relevant to the subjects, by providing clarifications for possible implications and by extending its application to society, business, industries, services, etc.

Course Construction: A curriculum and course design are intended to lay down the wider contours of a well-blended programme of theory, practice and social application prepared through a number of courses designed with details of specific objectives, teaching procedures, testing mechanism, teaching-learning materials to be used, co-curricular and extra-curricular activities to be organised, resources to be generated and follow-up work to be done including action research to be undertaken. It should suggest the different participatory roles of the teacher and the students to realise the overall goals.

Learning Resources: Institutions should possess adequate learning resources of different types and be made accessible to

ICT facilities should be available to all learners, such as laptops, ipods, ipads, etc provision of virtual learning is a matter of daily experience for the learner. Training should be provided to the teachers as well as the students in the skills to operate the modern technological tools of learning and use them for interaction teaching.

Faculty Improvement: Every institution should develop, year after year, in-house training programmes of its own for continuing faculty renewal. The training can be both general and specific. Similarly, the faculty should be liberally encouraged and incentivised to participate in further education programmes organised by institutions like the Academic staff colleges, other universities and colleges and corporate houses, NGO's, open universities and government departments. Faculty improvement programmes such as refresher courses, orientation courses are to be made available for the faculty with regular intervals.

Linkages with Society: Institutions can be linked purposefully with the society and its various agencies like business, finance, industries, media, social work, specific services, etc. The aim is to activise the knowledge developed in the classrooms and make it flow into various channels available to the society. MOUs can be entered into for specific purposes like student apprenticeship, assignments for work experience, part-time paid avenues of employment, research projects, awareness visits, etc. Inter-institutional collaboration can also be developed and continually expanded for sharing experience and expertise.

Co-curricular and Extra-curricular Activities: The activities that challenge different domains of the student's personality are very potent tools of adding value to the process of education of the whole man. Students are supposed to be both the actors and receivers of this process. The curricular and course designs mentioned earlier are intended to lay down the wide contours of the well-blended programme of theory, practice and social application. The institution should offer a very wide spectrum of co-curricular activities to choose from. And their implementation should involve goal-based evaluation, follow up and counselling to focus specific life skills and competences to be developed incrementally for the benefit of the society at large.

Performance Appraisal: Specific norms should be laid down and benchmarks be fixed for the development of personality of the students. Appraisal should be systematically done in these contexts. Their findings should be made public and analysed for future improvement. Necessary research should be undertaken to refine the processes involved. Their competencies have to be assessed through their performances.

Innovations: In India, for too long, higher education has been held captive to forces of obscurantism, ritualism, adhocism and myopia of perception and vision like rote learning, one-shot final external examination and ulterior considerations for declaring pass and fail categories. And all this is being done with unpardonable secrecy and unaccountability. It is high time the call for change and innovation in the teaching, learning practices being proclaimed by the irreversible forces of globalisation. Presently three innovations are on the cards. They are, one semesterisation of the academic year, two choice based credit system and three continuous internal evaluation through grading in place of the archaic marking system. In order to make higher education a value adding instrument of developing a holistic personality of the students, these innovations are unavoidable and found necessary. (Ghauchi, 2010)

Conclusion

With globalisation, the Indian Education System is facing new challenges in terms of competitions with not only the foreign institutes, but also from the private educational institutes. The new aims of education could be fulfilled with the changes and modification in education policies. The emphasis of new policies should be uni-culturisation, synthesisation and globalisation of education. Importance should be given to lifelong learning and self-learning. Generalisation of information should be given preference over summarisation of knowledge. New policies could be based on two perspectives: One is "Decentralised perspective" and other is "Need based perspective". The former talks about the distribution of power to the local authorities, the latter about the relevance of the policies for the actual 'Need Areas'. (Sam and Aroma, 2005)

3

ICTs in Integrated Education

Information Communication Technology (ICT) for Social Change

"The illiterate of the 21st century", according to futurist Alvin Taffler, "will not be those who cannot read and write, but those who cannot learn, unlearn and relearn". The International Labour Organisation defines the requirement for education and training in the new global economy simply as "Basic Education for All", "Core Work Skills for All" and Lifelong Learning for All". (ILO Report 2002).

Information and Communication Technologies (ICTs) have touched as potentially powerful enabling tools for educational change and reform. When used appropriately, different ICTs are said to help expand access to education, strengthen the relevance of education to the increasingly digital workplace, and raise educational quality by, among others, helping make teaching and learning into an engaging, active process connected to real life. However, the experience of introducing different ICTs in the educational settings all over the world suggests that the full realisation of the potential educational benefits of ICTs is not automatic. The effective integration of ICTs into the educational system is a complex, multifaceted process that involves not just technology-indeed, even enough initial capital, getting the technology is the easiest part: but also curriculum and pedagogy, institutional readiness, teacher competencies, and long term financing, among others. (Tinio, 2003)

In the 21st century, the explosion of knowledge has rendered the term 'up to date' outdated. Knowledge is changing so as that only 'up to-momentness' or up to-fraction of a moment' is in. In such a era only 'fit' societies or institutions, having an ability to 'adopt', 'adapt' and 'being adapt' would survive. In this context, ICTs can provide to be instrumental for survival, providing empowerment and equal distribution of opportunity. In recent years there has been a ground swell of interest in how computers and the internet can best be harnessed to improve the efficiency and effectiveness of education at all levels and in both formal and non-formal settings. Education means 'to draw out' facilitating realisation of self potential and latent talents of an individual. It is an application of pedagogy, a body of theoretical and applied research relating to teaching and learning that draws from different disciplines.

ICT education can be classified into four main categories in integrated higher education, such as, e-learning, U-learning, Blend learning and Distance learning.

e-Learning

Electronic learning (e-learning) is a general term used to computer enhanced learning. It is commonly associated with the field of Advanced Learning Technology (ALT), which deals with both the technology and associated methodologies in learning using networked and or multimedia technologies. It is also known as online learning. Distance education provides the base for e-learning for its development. e-learning can be 'on demand'. It overcomes time, distance, and travel constrains. (Muthuchamy and Thiyagu, 2010). Although most commonly associated with higher education and corporate, e-learning encompasses learning at all levels, both formal and non-formal that uses an information network-the Internet, an intranet (LAN) or extranet (WAN)-whether wholly or in part, for course delivery, interaction and facilitation. Others prefer the term 'online learning', Web-based Learning is a subset of e-learning and refers to learning using an Internet browser such as Netscape or Internet Explorer.(Tinio, 2003).

U-Learning

Ubiquitous Learning (U-learning) emerges through the concept of ubiquitous computing. U-learning means 'everywhere learning' (the internet or learning content follows people around). The core "knowledge pots" (work related content, personal knowledge, internet) hold content and information. Various devices plug in and retrieve the information in the appropriate format (PDA, cell phone, laptop, or any other technology gadgets). It fulfills e-learning's promise of "anytime, anywhere, and any context". After the initial impact and applications of computers in education, the introduction of e-Learning and mobile learning epitomised the constant transformation that were occurring in education. (Keegan, 2002)

Blended Learning

Blended Learning refers to learning models that combine traditional classroom practice with e-learning solutions. For example, students in a traditional class can be assigned both print-based and online materials, have online mentoring sessions with their teachers through chat, and are subscribed to a class e-mail list. Or a Web-based training course can be enhanced by periodic face-to-face instruction. "Blending" was prompted by the recognition that not all learning is best achieved in an electronically–mediated environment, particularly one that dispenses with a live instructor altogether. Instead, consideration must be given to the subject matter, the learning objectives and outcomes, the characteristics of the learners, and the learning context in order to arrive at the optimum mix of instructional and delivery methods. (Tinio, 2003)

Hybrid is a name commonly used to describe a class that combines fact to face classroom instruction with online learning. A major part of the activities take place online, while traditional classroom time is reduced but not eliminated. This type of class allows the students to have a more flexible schedule. It still allows for face to face contact with the instructor and classmate just like in a traditional class. Hybrid learning, sometimes called "Blend Learning", provides the best opportunities for learning transaction from classroom to e-learning. It provides students with an option of taking some learning materials fully online and some in class, or hybrid. These methods may include a mixture of face to face classrooms, self-placed learning and online classrooms. (Carmel, 2007)

Distance Leaning

Open and distance learning is defined by the common wealth of learning as "a way of providing learning opportunities that is characterised by the separation of teacher and learner in time or place or both time and place; learning that is certified in some way by an institution or agency; the use of a variety of media, including print and electronic; two way communications that allow learners and tutors to interact; the possibility of occasional face-to-face meetings, and a specialised division of labour in the production of delivery of courses." (The Commonwealth of Learning, 2002)

It is a type of education, where students work on their own at home or at the office and communicate with faculty and other students via e-mail, electronic forums, video conferencing, chat rooms, instant messaging and other forms of computer-based communication. This programme includes a Computer Based Training (CBT) system and communication tools to produce a virtual classroom. Because the internet and World Wide Web are accessible from virtually all the platforms, they serve as the foundation for many distance learning systems. (Littlejohn, Allison, *et al.*, 2009)

ICTs Access to Education

ICTs are a potentially powerful tool for extending educational opportunities, both formal and non-formal, to previously underserved constituencies scattered and rural populations, groups traditionally excluded from education due to cultural and social reasons such as ethnic minorities, girls and women, persons with disabilities, and the elderly, as well as all others who for reasons of cost or because of time constraints are unable to enroll on campus.

Anytime, anywhere: ICTs have the ability to transcend time and space. They make possible asynchronous learning, or learning characterised by a time lag between the delivery of instruction and its reception by learners. Additionally, certain types of ICTs, such as teleconferencing technologies, enable instruction to be received simultaneously by multiple, geographically dispersed learners (i.e., synchronous learners).

Teacher and the taught no longer have to rely solely on printed books and other materials in physical media housed in libraries for their educational needs. With the Internet and the World Wide Web (www), a wealth of learning materials in almost all the subjects and in a variety of media can now be accessed from anywhere and anytime by an unlimited number of people. They also facilitate access to resource persons-mentors, experts, researchers, professionals, businessmen and others all over the world.

ICTs can enhance the quality of education in several ways: by increasing learner motivation and engagement, by facilitating the acquisition of basic skills, and by enhancing teacher training. They are also transformational tools which, when used appropriately, can promote the shift to a learner-centreed environment. (Wadi and Sonia 2002)

Motivating to Learn

ICTs can be used to provide challenging and authentic content that will engage the students in the learning process. ICT, networked computers with internet connectivity can increase learners motivation as it combines the media richness and interactivity of other ICTs with the opportunity to connect with real people and to participate in world affairs.

Four Main Rationales for introducing ICTs in Education

Table 1

Rational	*Basis*
Social	Perceived role that technology now plays in society and the need for familiarising students with technology.
Vocational	Preparing students for jobs that require skills in Technology
Catalytic	Use of technology to improve performance and effectiveness in teaching, management and other social activities.
Pedagogical	To utilise technology in enhancing learning, flexibility and efficiency in curriculum delivery.

(Bhattacharya and Sharma 2007).

The use of ICT can improve students performance, teaching administration, and develop relevant skills in the disadvantaged communities. It also improves the quality of education by facilitating learning by doing, real time conversation self-learning, critical thinking, as well as the ability to communicate, collaborate and learn. Teaching and learning through ICT are underpinned by constructivist theories of learning and constitute a shift from a teacher-centred pedagogy to one of that is learner-centred.

Benefits of using ICTs in Education

Table 2 shows the main benefits of using ICTs in Education to various stakeholders. (Hadded and Jurich, 2002)

Table 2

Stakeholders	Benefits
Students	- Increased access
	- Flexibility of content and delivery
	- Combination of work and education
	- Learner-centred approach
	- Higher quality of education and new way of interaction.
	- Development of new learning culture.
Employers	- High quality, cost effective professional development in the work place.
	- Upgrading of employee skills, increased productivity.
	- Share of costs and of training time, with the employees.
	- Increased portability of training.
Governments	- To increase the capacity and cost effectiveness of education and training systems
	- To reach target group with limited access to conventional education and training.
	- To support and enhance the quality and relevance of existing educational structure.
	- To ensure the connection of educational institutions and curricula to emerging networks and information resources.
	- To promote innovation and opportunities for life long learning.

Transformation of Education through ICTs

Active Learning

ICT enhanced learning mobilises tools for examination, calculation and analysis of information, thus providing a platform for student inquiry, analysis and construction of new information. Learners therefore learn as they do and, whenever appropriate, work on in depth of real life problems, making learning less abstract and more relevant to the learner's life situation. In this way, and in contrast to memorisation based or rote learning, ICT enhanced learning is also "just in time" offering learners to choose what to learn when they need to learn it when their lives focus on the demand for such a study.

Collaborative learning

ICT supported learning encourages interaction and cooperation among students, teachers and experts regardless of where they are. Apart from modelling real world interactions, ICT supported learning provides learners the opportunity to work with people from different cultures, thereby helping to enhance learners' teaming and communicative skills as well as their global awareness. It models learning done throughout the learners' lifetime by expanding the learning space to include not just peers but also mentors and experts from different fields.

Creative Learning

ICT supported learning promotes the manipulation of existing information and creation of real–world products rather than the regurgitation of received information.

Integrative Learning

ICT enhanced learning promotes a thematic, integrative approach to teaching and learning. This approach eliminates the artificial separation between the different disciplines and between theory and practice that characterises the traditional classroom approach.

Evaluative Learning

ICT enhanced learning is student directed and diagnostic. Unlike static, text or point-based educational technologies, ICT enhanced learning recognises that there are many different learning pathways and many different articulation of knowledge. ICTs allow learners to explore and discover rather than merely listen and remember. (Bransford, 1999)

Stages of Teaching and learning with ICT

Teaching and learning process is interconnected and interrelated and hence cannot be separated. The process can be divided into four main stages:

Discovering ICT Tools

This initial stage focuses on discovery of new ICT tools by faculty and students. It is liked with the emerging approach in ICT development.

Learning how to use ICT Tools

In this second stage of teaching and learning process with the use of ICT. This stage emphasises on learning the use of new ICT tools. It involves the use of general or particular application of ICT.

Understanding how and when to use ICT Tools:

It focuses on understanding how and when to use ICT tools to achieve a particular purpose, such as in completing a given project. This stage indicates the ability to recognise situation where ICT will be helpful in choosing the most appropriate tools for a particular task, and using these tools in combination to solve real problem.

Specialising in the use of ICT Tools

The fourth stage involves specialising in the use of ICT tools. In this stage students study ICT as a specialised subject. Such a study concerns with vocational or professional education rather than general education. (Sharma, 1995).

The uses of ICTs in Education

Education policymakers and planners have to be clear about what educational outcomes are being targeted. These broad goals should guide the choice of technologies to be used and their modalities of use. The potential of each technology varies according to how it is used. Haddad and Drayler identify at least five levels of technology use in education: presentation, demonstration, drill and practice, interaction, and collaboration. (Haddad and Drayler, 2002)

Each of the different ICTs– print, audio/video cassettes, radio and TV broadcasts, computers or the Internet may be used for presentation and demonstration, the most basic of the five levels. Except for video technologies, drive and practice may be performed using the whole range of technologies. In the other hand, networked computers and the Internet are the ICTs that enable interactive and collaborative learning the best; their full potential as educational tools will remain unrealised if they are used merely for presentation or demonstration.

Issues in the use of ICTs in Education

Effectiveness, cost, equity, and sustainability are four broad intertwined issues which must be addressed when considering the overall impact of the use of ICTs in education. The educational effectiveness of ICTs depends on how they are used and for what purpose. And like any other educational tools or mode of educational delivery, ICTs do not work for everyone, everywhere in the same way. It is difficult to quantify the degree of which ICTs have helped expand access to basic education since most of the intentions for this purpose have been small scale and under-reported. In higher education and adult education there is some evidence that educational opportunities are being opened to individuals and groups who are constrained from attending traditional education. The use of computers, the internet and related technologies gives adequate teacher training and support, can indeed facilitate the transformation of the learning environment into a learner-centreed individual. (Fouts, 2002)

When considering whether ICT is "cost-effective" in educational selling, a definitive conclusion may not be possible for a variety of reasons. However, when considering the alternative of building more physical infrastructure, the cost savings to be realised from sharing resources, and the societal price of not providing access, ICTs as a means of enabling teaching and learning appears to be an attractive and necessary alternative. (Blurton, 2002)

In order to determine cost efficiencies, fixed cost, that is, retrofitting of physical facilities, hardware and networking software and upgrades and replacement, must be distinguished from variable costs, that is, professional development, connectivity including Internet access and telephone time, and maintenance and support, including utilities and supplies, and the balance between the two understood. If the fixed costs of technology projects are high and its variable costs are low, then there will be cost advantages to scaling up. Another dimension of cost is location, or who will pay for what. In projects that involve computers connected with Internet, either the school or student or both bear the variable costs. In contrast, with radio programming the learner has to pay only for a radio and a set of batteries. (Consortium for school Networking, 2002)

ICTs in education has made wide disparities between the rich and poor. It has widen divisions drawn among economic, social, cultural, geographic and gender lines. Ideally, one wishes for equal opportunity to participants. But access for different actors – both as users and producers – is weighted by their resources. Providing access to ICTs in education is only one facet of efforts to address equity issues. Equal attention must be paid to ensuring that the technology is actually being used by the target learners and in ways that truly serve their needs.

Cost and financing are not the only barriers to sustainability. The sustainability of ICT – based education programmes has four components: social, political, technological and economic. (Cisler, 2002)

Social sustainability is a function of community involvement. Innovation can happen only when all those who will be affected by it, whether directly or indirectly, know exactly why such an innovation is being introduced, what the implications are on their lives, and what part they can play in ensuring its success. ICT enabled education must serve the needs of the society.

Political sustainability refers to issues of policy and leadership. One of the biggest threats to ICT enabled education is resistance to change. If, teachers refuse to use ICTs in their classrooms, then use of ICTs can hardly take off, much less be sustained over the long term. Because of the innovative nature of ICT enabled education, leaders must have a keen understanding of the innovation process, identify the corresponding requirements for successful adoption, and harmonise plans and actions accordingly.

Technological sustainability involves choosing technology that will be effective over the long term. In a rapidly changing technology environment, this becomes a particular tricky issue as planners must contend with the threat of technological obsolescence. At the same time, there is a tendency to acquire only the latest technologies, when making technology decisions, planners should also factor in not just costs but also the availability of spare parts and technical support.

Economic sustainability or cost-effectiveness is the key, as technological investments typically run high and in many cases divert funds from other equally pressing needs. The need to develop multiple channels of financing through community participation ties economic sustainability closely to social and political sustainability.

Opportunities of Integrating ICTs in Education

Education Institutions have a mission to make teaching – learning process effective and interesting. ICTs integration in Education has a number of opportunities, such as, enhanced teaching-learning process, improved availability of study material; support for higher/distance education, and other remote areas.

ICT Research

ICT is needed in higher research and training to become world leader through its Doctoral Programmes. According to Vijayaraghavan, Founder of Technology park in Trivandrum, "We must be worried about the quantity, and relevance of knowledge generated by PhD. research. Run-of-the-mill research will generate degrees, not knowledge." Research in particular and education in general cannot be "pushed", rather it needs to be pulled by people capable of doing so. There is a lack of inspiration, and incentive today to induce an intelligent student to aspire for a doctoral research. To create the pull, the government and those who are in power can create an atmosphere to link the qualification for higher positions, not just based on experience, but making research degrees a prerequisite to attain them. These positions should be highly compensated, even more than industrial compensation. A large part of the compensations can be through incentives.

We have to aim at high quality research into :

1. The reality of the quality of today's ITC's manpower
2. The current and future needs of ITC industry
3. The solution to the quality problem
4. Capabilities in future ICT technology areas.

ICTs need holders of creative research degrees in areas such as Advanced Technology Research and Innovation Continuing Education 'skills' and re-skills' opportunities for employees within organisations; mentoring of entrepreneurs" (entrepreneurs within a company) and for driving a vibrant link between industry, intuition and research, and e-learning enhanced enrolment and examination process; increasing research activities. Traditional way of teaching-learning process can be enhanced by using ICTs. Teaching-learning process can be made more effective and interesting through this process. In the traditional learning system, learners and teachers are restricted to get knowledge on a particular topic through printed materials only. But the use of ICTs – facilitates them to get variety to study materials on a particular topic using Internet from anywhere and anytime. Print outs, audio, video, radio, T.V., computers and Internets are used to support distance education and e-learning. Enhanced enrolment and examination process can improve. The admission process is done through online. Education Institutions can also conduct examinations online. This will speed up admission and examination process. Application of ICTs in education enriches the research activities. More and more information about recent developments in different fields of study can be made available using Internet and appropriate software.

Challenges in Integrating ICTs in Education

Implications of ICT – enhanced Education

In spite of many benefits we learn from best practices around the world, there is no one formula for determining the optimal level of ICTs integration in the educational system. Some challenges may occur when policymakers and planners, educators, administrators and other stakeholders need to utilise educational policy planning, infrastructure, language, content, capacity building and financing.

Educational policy planning to enhance and reform education through ICTs require clear and specific objectives, guidelines and time bound targets, mobilisation of required resources, and the political commitment at all levels to see the initiative through. Some of the elements of planning for ICTs are: Factors needed, that is, drivers and barriers to ICTs use need to be identified, including those related to curriculum and pedagogy, infrastructure, capacity building, language, content and financing. The specification of educational goals at different education and training levels as well as the different modalities of use of ICTs that can best be employed in pursuit of these goals. This requires the policy makers in understanding the potentials of different ICTs when applied in different contexts for different purposes, and an awareness of priority for education needs and financial and human resource capacities and constraints within the context. Even the best designed models those that have already been proven to work in other contexts need to be tested on a small scale first. Such pilot studies are essential to identify, and correct, potential glitches in institutional design, implementability and effectiveness.

Infrastructure-related challenges in ICT enhanced Education

Appropriate infrastructure, buildings, extensive retrofitting to ensure proper electrical wiring, ventilation, safety and security would be needed. Another basic requirement is the availability of reliable supply of electricity. Policy makers should also look at the ubiquity of different types of ICT in the context in general and in the educational system in particular. A basic requirement for computer-based or online learning is access to computers in educational institutions, communities, and households, as well as affordable Internet service. (Hawkins, 2002)

Challenges with respect to Capacity Building

There are number of competencies to be developed throughout the educational system for ICT integration to be successful. Faculty development is of primary importance.

There should be development of skills with particular application; integration into existing curricula; curricular changes related to the use of ICT., changes in teachers' role, and underpinning educational theories. (MacDougall, *et al.* 1997). With the introduction of ICTs in Education, the role of teachers in the learning process becomes even more critical. The role of students, in turn, also expands. Since ICT teaching can be extended to outside world, the community can also play a new role in education. As learning shifts from the "teacher-centred model" to a "learner-centred model", the teacher becomes less the sole voice of authority and more the facilitator, mentor and coach. Teacher's role rise in encouraging students to involve in learning, to ask questions and pose problems, formulate hypotheses, collect information and critically assess the information for hypotheses testing. Teachers become co-learners and discover new things along with their students.

Administration and Technical Support

In education administration plays a key role for the development of integration of ICTs. Some of the teacher or student–initiated ICTs have been undermined by lack of support from academic administrators. For ICT integration programmes to be effective and sustainable administrator themselves must be competent in the use of the technology, and they must have a broad understanding of the technical, curricular, administrative, financial, and social dimensions of ICT use in education. While the technical support requirements of an institution depend ultimately on what and how technology is deployed and used, general competencies that are required would be in the installation, operation, and maintenance of technical equipment, network administration, and network security. Without on-site technical support, much time and money may be lost due to technical breakdown.

Content Developers

Another critical area that is too often overlooked is Content Development. The bulk of existing ICT based integrated material is mostly in English. There is a need to develop original educational content, namely, radio programmes, interactive multimedia learning materials on CD–Rom or DVD, Web-based Courses, etc., adopting existing content, and convert print-based content to digital media. These are tasks for which content development specialists, programmers, multimedia course authors, and web-developers are needed. Like technical support specialists, content developers are highly skilled professionals and are not, with the exception of instructional designers, historically employed by institution and distance education programmes and those who otherwise make use of ICTs, have dedicated technical support and content development units. (Tinio, 2003)

Impact of ICT Integration in Integrated Education

The impersonality, suppression of communication, mechanisms, elimination of peer-to-peer learning, reduced social and cultural interactions are major impediments associated with ICT Education. It cannot replace human brain or human beings creative function. ICT Education has the challenge to "bride the knowledge gap", in terms of improving quality education. Increasing the quantity and quality of educational opportunities, making knowledge power through borderless and boundless accessibility to resources and people even in remote areas to satisfy their basic right to education is a formidable task to achieve. As various ICTs become increasingly affordable, accessible and interactive their role at various levels of education is all the more significant in making educational outcomes relevant to the content, is revolutionising educational content and delivery, and fostering "information literacy".

There is a world wide need felt for integrating ICT into education in order to improve the pedagogy that reflect a social change. The main goals of ICT adoption and integration in the field of education are reducing the cost per student, making education more affordable and accessible, increasing the enrollments of learners, improving course content, and meeting the needs of various stakeholders. The main factors that affect the adoption of ICT integrated education are the mission or goal in a particular contest, programme and curriculum, teaching-learning strategies, learning techniques, learning material and resources, communication and interaction, support and delivery system, students, faculty and experts infrastructure, administration and evaluation. Coherent strategies and actions are the most important factors in integrating ICT in education. Cost and maintenance are other important issues that decide and guide the adoption and growth of ICT in Education. Along with ICT training and updating, one needs an ICT related support mechanism to gradually induce the integration. Teachers need support in using and integrating ICT in curriculum development practice, and teaching. Teachers and learners who perceive greater ICT related exposure and support will perform better. Changes in curricula do support fundamental economic and social transformation of the society. Such transformations require new kind of skills, capabilities and attitudes which can be developed by integrating ICT in education.

The use of laptops by students, both in urban and rural areas will enhance ICT based learning. Students can get benefited from connectivity to Educational Multimedia Research Centres, Gyan Vision and other sources. Teaching learning process will have more transparency by way of online valuation. There will be resistance to any new initiative, but once it is pilot-tested, there will be wide acceptance, such an initative must be implemented in phases, considering the integrity of the education system, proper training for the teachers and faculty are vital for industry institute interface. Awareness initiatives by educational institutions will take the entire process to a higher level.

4

Ethics and Values in Integrated Education

Inculcating Value in Integrated Education

Education is a powerful and pervasive agent for all round development of individual and social transformation. For Gandhiji, the true meaning of education is harmonious development of head, heart and hand, i.e., enlightenment of mind, compassion and dignity of labour. For Radhakrishnan, "moral and spiritual training is an essential part of education". Swami Vivekananda had proclaimed: "We must have life-building, man-making, and character building education." For him "Education for values should be education for man-making and character building. Values like co-operation, tolerance, neighbourliness, austerity and so on should be exercised in right earnest in the continual course of education".

According to Shankar Dayal Sharma, "The aim and objective of all education is to maintain, sustain and develop a healthy mind in a healthy body." Shankar Dayal Sharma had said, "Thus a teacher must succeed in conveying the larger ideals of service to the community, virtues of tolerance and respect for all faiths, the importance of character, integrity and discipline and the value of humanism to his pupils. They should be also made aware of our heritage and culture." Pundit Nehru said, "A vast responsibility... rests on our educational institutions and those who guide their destinies. They have to keep their lights burning and must not stray from the right path even when passion convulses the multimedia and blinds many amongst those whose duty is to set example to others."

Rabindranath Tagore had a vision for education: "Education must aim at the development of moral, spiritual and ethical values and we should seek them in our own heritage as well as in other cultures and civilisations..." As per Confucius, human beings are teachable, improvable and perfectible through personal and communal endeavour especially including self cultivation and self-creation. The main idea of Confucianism is the cultivation of virtue and the development of moral perfection. (Ping-cheung 1999)

Ours is a land of the Buddha and Mahatma Gandhi, and it is supposed to be a land of truth and non-violence, but as Dalai Lama once observed, much of non-violence has been exported to other countries and there is violence here. Times are hard for the student community of our country and the policy makers for higher education have an urgent task of redeeming the youth from commercialising of education and the mechanical academic life. Such a time education values therefore, necessitates and harmonises the essential components contributing to the growth and development of personality.

Creation of the right environment, which helps and encourages young minds to resolve personal and moral issues independently is of utmost importance. The greatest challenge the world is facing today, is the crisis of confidence and character, mental and moral decay and break down of traditional discipline. True knowledge consists of self-understanding and self-control. If education has to serve the humanity and ameliorate human suffering, it must teach and train us to respect each other (universal brotherhood), love each other (Universal love) and to practice compassion and to uphold the dignity of all lives. In a world which is primarily torn between a few 'haves' and majority of 'have nots', diversities, self-centred vision, violence, terrorism and consumerism are creating a dreadful scenario. In this chaotic atmosphere 'value-based education' is the only hope for synthesising the moral fabric of individual and generating a culture of peace in the society. (Sinha, 2002)

Value Based Integrated Education

The Gurus believed that education was a process in Gurukulas where the students developed into respectable citizens. They taught the students values, which guided them to a healthy and harmonious social living. The Gurus believed that human values were what the students should live by and what they would die for. The Gurus were convinced that providing the students with the knowledge and skills that would enable them to realise their professional aspirations were only a part of their education; the more important part was making them young citizens of values, culture and patriotism. Each generation of society passes on its social heritage and cultural tradition to the next generation, which is known as the transmission of culture. The Gurus prepared the students to face the challenges of career and life by inculcating in them values of the culture and developing in them a positive attitude. (Sundararajan, 2002)

The popular concept of modern day education, particularly higher education, has adversely changed with the main objective of passing the examinations with good marks and giving a few vocational skills to fit into a job. But modern education has ignored the heart, it has ignored the fact that students are a subject matter of immense significance both for the present and the future of their country. The engineers, doctors, scientists, economists, teachers and others advocate in the name of modernisation, look for materialistic progress. Change and materialistic development alone do not signify human progress and the progress of the society. Again there is a limit for the humans to absorb changes and materialistic development. The youth have become the victims of over vaulting materialistic ambition and unknowingly have accelerated the pace of their life. The result is gastric neurosis, mental disorder and behavioral problems.

Unfortunately, the meaning of education generally in the 21st century, is teaching the youth to live by machines and gadgets and not by the universal human values like truth, non-violence, love and compassion. These values are relegated and man is fast becoming a non-entity. The young men want to be always busy with their business and industry, which can multiply their money. Leisure and social get-together are generally neglected. The result is obvious, the family and society breaking away. When values are forsaken, chaos overtakes order. The present way of thinking, behaviour and life are changing so adversely that there is now an urgency to make value education an integral part of education.

Computer Information systems and other modern Information and Communication Technology have so advanced that we cannot wait any longer for any natural process to redeem the youth from the commercialised way of functioning and artificial way of living. Life has become so artificial and materialistic that young men and women have begun to think whether they need any value system at all that will guide them to the right way of living. If this doubt becomes a conviction, life will not be human, and our society cannot be called a humane society.

The fast pace of life and madness for money have been badly mistaken for 'progress' and the youth are already in the grip of frenzy for such a kind of progress. They are obsessed with such 'progress' that they do not know what to speak to others, and what they can give to others. There is always a sense of urgency with everybody. They are tense even when they do not do anything; perhaps they are worried that they are not doing anything in that particular hour. Impatience is becoming the ruling principle and men and women want to work even when they are physically exhausted. They are particular to keep themselves busy even when it is unnecessary. They think it is below their dignity to take the company of men who work slowly and leisurely.

The resultant anxiety has led to an unhealthy competition in the academic world, and in the business world and leading to crimes and violence in the political world. Integrity in character, public manners and social controls are breaking down. Life has become a rate-race and completing the tasks before the dead line has become the ruling phrase. Man is looked at as a multi-functioning machine, not as a valuable organic being. There is always a tension between man and time as he wants to make prosperity out of it, resulting in stress, anxiety and breakdown of health. There are of course the more alarming consequences. Materialistic development and crimes have begun to grow together. Technology goes handy to the criminals and often we hear about high-tech cheating, high-tech forgery and high-tech-serial killing. The youth live in a country where hatred grows in the name of religion, crimes are politicised, and violence is mistaken for nationalism, separatist forces try to give refuge to the unemployed but aggressive youth. (Sundararajan, 2002)

Objectives of the Policy for Value Based Education are:

- to instill in the youth, a deep awareness and respect for the principles enshrined in the constitution and a willingness to further the rule of law with commitment to national identity, integration, non-violence, secularism and socialism.
- to promote awareness of the cultural heritage with a commitment to their preservation as well as enrichment of their environment and ecology.
- to develop qualities of discipline, self-reliance, justice and fairplay, sporting spirit, concern for public welfare and scientific temper to combat superstition, obscurantism and such social evils.
- to provide maximum access to education for personality development as well as vocational training.
- to make the youth aware of international issues and to involve them in promoting peace and understanding for a just economic order. (Youth Policy, 1988)

Yoga and meditation discipline the five senses and allow reason to work. They help the students to affirm the facts and choose their activities. They develop in them an ability to act with freedom and confidence. Inter-religious dialogues are necessary for our pluralistic society. The youth should know that religion is for man and not man for religion. The ultimate purpose of any religion can be to elevate man to the state of a saint. If any religion breeds hatred it cannot be a religion at all.

Communication skills prove to be an important tool for the youth to absorb value education and conduct programmes on it, in and out of the campus. Debate is an excellent art of communication that sharpens the intellect of a student. Gyles Brandreth (1984) comments on debate thus, "For the inexperienced and nervous speaker, one of the best ways of learning the art of public speaking and conquering fear is to take part in debate. Debating encourages quick thinking and gives valuable practice in putting thoughts into words in front of an audience. Debate teaches the participants self-discipline and it helps them to discover their merits and inadequacies. Group discussions, debates and practice sessions of public speaking should be conducted in the campuses on the erosion caused to values in modern life. These great arts of communication teach the youth first discipline, as discipline is doing something, which does not come easily. It is practice of a chosen profession with commitment and conscience that can make somebody excel in it." A disciplined person is not a rigid person and he takes care of himself. He knows discipline is forming the right habits for a harmonious living, it is not self-negation.

Teachers should aim to inculcate discipline, which will help students when they enter different fields and work with their fellow beings with love. It will help them to lead a collective and harmonious life. Students must be encouraged to know the greatness of love and must be influenced to associate themselves with the object of love towards their fellowmen. It is the activities on value based education that teach the youth the principle that personal integrity is more important than company manners. It is value based education that gives their life a concrete direction, meaning and profundity. The values shape their inner sense of what is right and what is wrong. Values are not laws but they are principles that show a person who he is. It is in the light of values the youth should make the hard choices in life. When they make the right choice, they should act with integrity, honesty, courage and generosity.

Value based education teaches the youth that knowledge and skills are not the only requisites to succeed in life, but a positive attitude and a humane way of action. Values teach the youth to laugh at their miseries and be sympathetic towards others miseries. Men with values and independent thinking do not succumb to pressures from time and their competitors. They take their competitors as a group of which they are good members or good leaders. Men of values and independent thinking do not think they are above the competitors. They do not think themselves to be leaders with special gifts. (Purushothaman and Stella 1995)

Value based education teaches harmony, independence and leadership. A person who succeeds in the right way, he is one who inspires others to succeed. He appreciates others' problems too and tells them how to solve them. We should remember that our children, the future generation, start from only where we end.

Education is for life, not for a living. It must provide the individual, the wherewithal to face the challenges and find meaning and fulfillment in life. There are only two lasting bequests we can hope to give our children – one of these is roots, the other, wings. The roots symbolise the cultural and spiritual moorings that we must provide to the young so that they cultivate inner strength to face the vicissitudes of life and are not carried away easily by the winds of worldly storms and tempests. The wings represent the capacity to dream that the sky is the limit for our achievements and the ability to realise our dreams in our own lifetime. Education must serve both ends. (Sahini, 2007)

Values and Higher Education

The consequences of an education system devoid of values are reflected in the following poignant letter by a survivor of a concentration camp set up during World War II:

Dear Teacher

> *I am a survivour of a concentration camp. My eyes saw what no man should witness – gas chambers built by learned engineers, children poisoned by educated physicians, infants killed by trained nurses, women and babies shot and burnt by high school and college graduates.*
>
> *So, I am suspicious of education. My request to you is: help your students become human. Your efforts should never produce learned monsters, skilled psychopaths, educated eichmanns. Reading, writing and arithmetic are important only if they serve to make our children more human." (Narasimhamurty, 2005)*

Analogy: Analogy involves the use of drawing parallels between two similar themes. For instance, in banking, there are three important ways of securing funds from the bank-drawing against a deposit, raising an advance against the security of properties and securing the guarantee of a wealthy person acting as surety. Similarly, in life there are three ways to become eligible for divine grace. That is, if we have practiced on daily life good thoughts, good words and good deeds, it is like the deposit in the savings bank account against which withdrawls are permitted in times of need. Our parents, ancestors might have done a lot of good. These are like the accumulated properties against which divine succour may be sought. If neither option is feasible, we could secure a Guru to act as our guarantor. Who is the Guru? Faith is our Guru. Faith in oneself and faith in God is the secret of success. (Sahni, 2007)

Religion – Spiritual Aspect Of Integrated Education

The relevance of religiosity has a special place especially in the modern scientific age as of today. Unlike the past, the 21st century modernity is a stirring and disturbing period for all essential and fundamentalist presuppositions so far. To some persons, it is precisely seeking the relevancy of religion vis-à-vis the march of scientific quest of man. For some others, it is to question its relevance in the context of socio-economical developments as pursued today. Basically the spiritual call of man hints at the higher and unspeakable, unknown and mysterious goals for man beyond any rationalisation. As a matter of fact it has doubtlessly remained as a central aspiration for man throughout. For, despite all secular lures for material goods and objectivities presently notwithstanding, this core challenge for the spiritual hunger of the higher goal as intrinsically unique to human identity in some way or the other, has also driven man religiously. It is this latter continuity of hunger till now, definable or undefinable as though has been mainly a path of spiritual pilgrimage through various religious perspectives. It is to constantly understand and realise this inner exploratory process by man. An apparent collective belonging to some religion is one thing whereas gauging the place of this utmost democratic process within every human being is another thing. That is why instead of apparent comparing and contrasting various scriptural schemata and beliefs as followed traditionally, it is better to probe this rationale of the inmost religious quest by man as such.

To restate, granting all distinct manifestations of forms of Divine beliefs and varieties of practical expressions, it is mainly the spiritual hunger for the higher goals, a leaping into realising and relating to the superior relationship of oneself with the transcendental being in some way or the other remains the central force in the religio-spiritual pursuit as such. It may be agreed that man is not always and everywhere rationally circumspect in probing this deeper spiritual self-identity. Moreover, he is yet very far in universalising and culturising this unique aspiration on the anvil of self-analysis and experiencing the same. May be for centuries man is habitually cultivated and leaning for certain external objectivities and intentional exterior goals rationally and all multi-formed religious beliefs and visions have yet to awaken man fully to the basic spiritual challenges in each human person universally. To reiterate, man is still confined to the status of religious externals and all its outer self-identities very much indeed. As a corollary, when the modernity being threadbare critique in nature, raises fundamental questions regarding the place of religiosity today. This is 'openly reflected in the psyche of insecurities' and fearing calls by all religions vis-a-vis all-pervasive materialistic lures of life and deeper identities with secular developments by mankind presently. (Cousins, 1971).

The Nature and Scope of Spirituality

Some basic queries in this inquiry are: What do we mean when we think about spirituality in the religious realm? What is its constitution? What are the goals aimed by it? Ontologically the subject of religion is abstract and unscrutable in nature, it is but natural to examine its functional process taking place within man rather than the ontological quest of the idea of spirituality. The religious perspective means it is a certain nature of action by man not dependent on any materialist bearing as such. To some it is an impelling for a higher and impersonal ideal, some may identify it with emotional and aesthetic development of man. To some it suggests as aiming to lead oneself to higher and higher goals of human life. After-all it is a unique human metaphysical search of self-transcendence which is not to be confused with as non-secular as it is a very much secular human experience. It is an action which does not look beyond itself for meaning and validity. It is a process of collective human search for higher intrinsic values, an inner dialectical process constantly goading man for higher and fuller views of truth, beauty and goodness. Thus, it is a deeper human experiential fact that despite all possessions of physical, mental and moral well-being, man does have a constant sense of inadequacy everywhere. All religions therefore call and direct man in readily striving by submitting and surrendering himself to a call of superior reality, in leading him to better perfecting state of spiritual existence as a unique human person. (Cousins, 1971)

Spirituality as Distinct from Morality

The pertinent problem comes up as to how the moral action differs from spiritual action. For like spirituality, moral action too means striving for an ideal. However, the later moral system takes for granted the finite constitution of man. It is characterised by human limitation and expects disciplined unity accordingly. As against this, the pursuit of spirituality is a process of minimising the limitation of the efforts of man. The spirituality reveals the deeper side of human personality. Despite all conditional limitations of man externally, it is still an open way for the greater and unknown potentialities of self. In reality ethics derives its values from spirituality; else the ethical aim would be a mere tolerating self-interest. (Whitehead, 1933)

Spirituality as Distinct from Science

The basis of science is that of free inquiry. It is uniquely a questioning pursuit for 'truth' bearing a committed intention and verification of the same. The dynamism rooted in it symbolises the period of modernity which is shaking all time-old dogmas, opinions, etc. This has been very much reflected in man's unprecedented mental and material progress as of today. Not only that, it has dealt a deadly blow to all closely held religious beliefs so far, compelling all religions to reassess its meaning and scope so as to suit with its spirit of inquiry as such. Its approach consists in collecting relevant data in all disciplines of knowledge and making for an objective interpretation of the same.

There are limitations in the scope of morality but it does not imply that the concept of morality is limited. In the same way the various aspects of science are limited but that does not convey that the spirit of scientific inquiry is limited in nature. As against this, the spiritual process is a ceaseless quest in the search of the mystery of the inner reality which guides and moulds the total existential reality of man. Unlike the stark approach of particularity in science relating the man with the 'known', the subtle holistic approach of spirituality strives in relating the man with the 'unknown'. It is a sublime attitude and thought as a unified view of mental life of man. Both realms of knowledge have distinctly a vast and wide scope aiming at 'truth' and they need not be reduced to one another. At the same time a close relationship between them becomes the foundation of all human knowledge and the hope for the future.

The spiritual unity of matter, life, mind, reason and spirit at variegated differential macrocosmic spheres, is a fact of the integral, unitive, intuitive microcosmic sphere within human experiences. For all religions, it is a way of removing all impurities and imperfections. To all religions, the root power is human self or consciousness. Apparently the religions may look different and contradictory as though, there is a deeper vitality in converging on the anvil of spiritual striving. It only means that the religious practices and organisational goals should not remain routinely static and restrictive as convenient tools in the name of true religiosity. (Vyas, 2010)

Moral Dilemmas in the Era of Globalisation

One of the features of human history has been that people, resources, ideas including knowledge and values move from one place to another and in the era of globalisation these are moving all too fast and getting transformed vigorously. The basic questions are: what is the role of values in such movements and transformations? Is our identity-ethnic and linguistic – getting lost in the process of globalisation? Or does globalisation enhance people's sensitivity to their moral values and to transform their attitudes to other values? Is it really the stage of human history known as the end of ideology and the end of nationality? Is globalisation an encroachment of the dominant moral values and culture of the West upon other cultures? These are some of the most basic questions that are frequently asked.

Origin of globalisation involves economic factors with trade and finance, liberalisation, linked trade technology, political and moral situations helping it. Globalisation may be defined as "universalisation, internationalisation, liberalisation, westernisation and deteritorisation. There are four dimensions involved in the formulation and implementation of the policies towards globalisation. These are the neo-liberals, the reformists, the radicals and the revolutionaries. There are certain imminent consequences of globalisation, such as the end of state, the end of modernity, ideologies and the end of nationality, etc. It is in this context that moral dilemmas arise affecting both the aspects of moral and values, i.e. the relative and the universal. Globalisation has the twin function to perform, namely to enhance people's sensitivity to their moral values and to transform their attitudes to other values. A moral dilemma arises when we are confronted with equally valid moral alternatives.(Robertson, 1992).

What gives globalisation its unending fascination and eternal relevance are the moral dilemmas that everybody faces, being constantly confronted by equally valid alternatives. Ronald Robertson argues that the globalisation is 'the interpenetration of the universalisation of particularisation and the particularisation of universalism" (Robertson, 1992). Moral dilemmas arise only in this process of the fusion of the universal and the particular. It presents irreconcilable alternatives and the choice between them seems to be made irrationally or for reasons other than moral. The well-known example is that globalisation is by no means uniform; it always means different things to different people. And there are sufficient moral grounds to justify or to reject certain choices. For some, globalisation means media, rapid transmission of messages and symbols. For others, it is a deregulation of domestic as well as external markets – goods and services. It appreciates the total capital market with the need to promote investment. This is done with Cyber Space and the Internet. It can describe the expansion of economic activities across ethnicity and identity, values and practices and even beyond national boundaries. This later on is converted into trade and commerce, banking, rural institutions and so on. All these are necessary beyond the state because globalisation means global banking, trade and commerce, global migration of population, etc. All these require certain rules, institutions and the infrastructures, which can go beyond nation state. So we have organisations like WTO, GATS, new definitions of the UNO and other UNO funded organisations. With these institutional mechanisms, global reality is regulated and managed. Globalisation also has structural pre-requisites and imperatives. One such imperative is that people will 'move' and with them there will be a movement of consciousness and values. (Singh, 2010)

Morals and conceptions of good are said to be relative to cultures, even large cultural identities have now disintegrated into smaller ones – cultural pluralism. Pluralism and tolerance are the ethos of globalisation. State can certainly and strongly find and frame rules and institutions for governance to provide enough space for local identities, communities and environmental resources to ensure globalisation. Re-defining such values as in the adopting of human rights and setting development goals on environment, population, social development, etc. globalisation should be with regard for pluralistic value systems without violation of human rights. Without marginalising local identities, the reward of globalisation should be toward creating equity or equality between nations. (Hume, 2002)

Values and Virtues in the Era of Globalisation

The ethical nature of academics bifurcates in two directions: that which values impress upon society or people, and that which virtues can actually establish as part of change. Today not much reference is made to virtues, but we do refer a lot to values. The fundamental difference between virtues and values stems from the fact that the former (virtues) belong to the subject's environment and the latter (values) belong to the object's environment. Victor Garcia Hoz supports this difference between virtues and values when he states that we can talk about the "values of things" and "human values", "We should not forget that the value of truth, among others, is inherent in the birth of universities." (Vid *et al.,* 1995) We could call the second category "virtues". In other words, when a value incorporates human conduct as an energy that leads to the "incarnation" of this value, we may refer to its corresponding virtue. To illustrate this point, we could say that truth is a value; its acquisition by a human being produces the virtue of "veracity". Put another way, the value is the objectification of the content of a virtue.

Virtues normally conjure up this ideal image of human beings, namely, an ethical approach based on the highest attainable level. However, values, which are purely objective, do not involve the incorporation of a theory of mankind and its perfection. On the other hand, values are most pertinent when one does not refer to human beings, but to institutions. If we view the ethical environment of universities as institutions, it would seem logical to refer to values and not virtues as an initial observation. However, institutions are not simply comprised of throngs or great masses of individuals, but rather communities of people.

The distinction between virtues and values and their inclusion in the ethical vision of academic institutions gives rise to two principles: that values are taught and that virtues are practiced. Not paying enough attention to either of these two fields will lead to a lack of symmetry, which will leave gaps in institutional ethical practice. The reality of certain values being taught without taking into consideration their counterparts, that is, in not putting virtues into practice, results in an abstract theory that does not motivate people from an existential point of view. There should be an adequate balance or point of convergence between theory and practice. The synthesis between the teaching of values and the implementation of virtues is thus part of the anthropological reasoning behind this theory. (Rubio, 2004)

Sobrinho states that "There are values that are common to higher education on a global level: the search for truth, ethics, respect for diversity, scientific rigor, autonomy, freedom of thought, the culture of peace, self-criticism, etc." (IESALC-UNESCO-2008).

The search for truth is therefore one of the integral values of the academic experience. Providing integrated education involves knowing beforehand what the key dimensions of human beings are and what aspects are considered relevant education in general have primarily sought to develop cognitive skills. Students have to put into practice values at various levels, for example, team work, responsibility, discipline, organisation skills and inter personal skills and so on. However, one is also able to see the unfolding of a student's ethical development. This is because the relationship that has been established with one's peers and with one's work enables a student to develop on an ethical, spiritual and personal level through constant interaction and practical laboratory type activities.

To speak of ethics and values at academic institutions to science and academic disciplines implies that they begin with human experience. First of all, there is need for man to obtain virtues from values in such a way that institutions become an environment where social harmony and ethical maturity thrive. Ethical reflection should begin with approaching both the discussion of current theories and the applications relevant to methodologies by uniting the practice of values in establishing meaning and developing enquiry of the recent interpretations of reality. Ethics, values and virtues should be present in the education mission, so that their institutional pertinence may be evident. In this sense, one needs to establish the search for truth as a core value in addition to integral training (that is rooted in a spiritual and a psychosomatic understanding of human beings), plus the development of a practical science and the design of creative forms of service to society. (Aide, 2010)

Development of Holistic Knowledge

The roles of private trusts and organisations started with the noble idea of service to society. Most of them, excepting a few exceptions, end up as profit making institutions compromising on quality, encouraging corruption and nepotism, producing sub standard and incompetent human resource, which speaks volumes not only about the receding quality in education, which directly affects the economic, social and cultural life of ... but also question the validity of our delivery system.

Apart from competence, corruption, paucity, scarcity of innovative ideas, lack of drastic reforms in education sector and particularly higher education, paucity of funds, lack of students for certain traditional courses, lack of infrastructural facilities, lack of vision, lack of leadership and influence of demagogue politics in educational institutions, interference of external forces and last but not the least, in this long list is the lack of enthusiasm among students to inculcate value based education. Our educational system does not provide an opportunity for holistic knowledge, we either produce defective and substandard human intellect or produce highly specialised, subject-specific grounded persons. We have to bring drastic reforms in our educational system by introducing choice based credit system, which paves the way for an integrated approach. Unfortunately, the Ministry of Human Resource Development of the Government of India is yet to concentrate on these vital sectors. Our education should be relevant to our society, culture, and country. (Shivkumar, 2009)

Development of Holistic Personality

The role of education is to culture the individual in such a manner that he himself lives blissfully and also contributes to the society in its progress and peace. Education today reached the level of producing good programmers for computer programming but is not able to provide the technology to programme ones mind – the most powerful cosmic computer to lead a balanced and progressive life in a positive manner.

The present day education is giving a world of information about various things but does not give education to nurture one's own self, thereby causing incompleteness and dissatisfaction. Knowledge of the knower is missing in the present process of education. True education is not just giving the bundle of books and information about virtues and values in life but to culture the mind, body, intellect, speech and senses in such a manner that the individual lives life in enlightenment, free from mistakes, enjoying knowledge, power and bliss. The segmented and fragmented experience of studying separate disciplines and specialising in an academic field without the experience of the wholeness of knowledge and the wholeness of life, not only fails to develop the brain's potential but it actually hinders the development of the mature intellect and personality by directing student's attention only to partial values of knowledge. The teaching of yoga, meditation and the ancient Indian disciplines can help in achieving this objective of educating the people to understand their self and develop holistic personality.

Most often maintaining and promoting the culture is understood in terms of folk arts, music, dance, etc., just for entertainment without connecting and inspiring the real cultural values which uphold the individual and social life of the land. The need for value based education has been felt realising the fact that in spite of great scientific advancement and information explosion, the life of highly educated people, many a times are found to be neither good for themselves nor for the society.

Scientists explore the hidden laws of nature. The laws of nature are innumerably infinite and even though it is not possible to remember all the laws of nature all the time by everyone, it is possible to tune our thoughts and actions to the laws of nature through the technologies of consciousness. Settled silent level of individual's consciousness being the state of perfect order, all the universal values become lively in the thought and action of the individual through the experience of transcendental consciousness. It gives the ability to spontaneously act in accordance with the law of nature, ability to maintain harmony and life supportive action at global or even cosmic level without loosing the local values the individual gains the ability to have progress while simultaneously contributing to the progress of society and evolution without holding or causing obstruction to the progress of others.

"If we are really sincere in our approach to develop value based education, the time has come to practically use the scientifically validated techniques of our great Vedic tradition." We see in society today that talking about the values and teaching them in curriculum have not been able to create an ideal citizen or an ideal society. Education has to be based on universal values, values that keep the whole cosmos progressive and evolving in a smooth manner in spite of great diversities. We have to be conscious of developing and evolving consciousness to imbibe these universal values in the conscious awareness of the individual. (Sharma, 2010)

The enduring survival and the pursuit of revival of higher education values across time and culture are anchored on critical dimensions characterised by the socio-cultural orientation, political form of government, religion, economic growth, development, inherent traditional practices, vision and mission. We have been witnessed to these values, which have penetrated and integrated through our system of education. The succinct analysis of these selected values in the above mentioned discussion provides insights on how education system is influenced and affected. Apparently, there are advantages and disadvantages, benefits and risks, challenges and issues, threats and weakness, limitations and opportunities, which would require strong advocacy and dissemination of the outcomes to people who are responsible in promoting higher education. Each stakeholder has a vital role to play for enhancing and enabling these values to make sustainable impact on the diverse learning environments and landscapes. The students, as consumers of education, have to be vigilant in asserting their demands and requirements, which result to create and discover new horizons and strategies which would make these values more meaningful and functional. The rising expectations and aspirations of the people is also a determinant that trigger the modifications, innovations, improvement and revision of intents, contents and approaches of these educational values.

The dynamic leadership and governance of both public and private education institutions likewise play a vital role in the survival and revival of values which are deemed relevant and responsive to the needs of the academic community. Lastly, the governments regardless of forms or structures have the primary responsibility to ensure that these values are put in place to ensure access and quality in education for its people by appropriating funds and resources where these are needed most. Proper orientation, well-defined vision and platform of the political leaders can make the difference for the survival and revival of these values. The international organisations can likewise advocate the appropriate values to help sustain education in general and higher education in particular throughout the world. The credibility, the suitability and applicability of these values are all in our hands. Let us face the challenge together by integrating the values, virtues and ethics in the education system.

5

Curriculum for Integrated Education

Concept of Integrated Curriculum

In an Integrated approach the curriculum of a programme cuts across subject-matter lines. It brings a meaningful association of various views, perspectives and features. It focuses upon broad areas of study. It underscores learning and teaching in a holistic way. It focuses upon comprehensive life problems. Integrated approach reflects the real world and is interactive. (Lake, 1993)

The term that is often used synonymously with integrated curriculum is interdisciplinary curriculum. Interdisciplinary curriculum is defined in the Dictionary of Education as, "a curriculum organisation which cuts across subject-matter lines to focus upon comprehensive life problems or broad based areas of study that brings together the various segments of the curriculum into meaningful association." (Good,1973) 'Interdisciplinary' can attain throughout each of school subjects... Synergistic teaching does more than integrate: it presents content and skills in such a manner that nearly all learning takes on new dimensions, meaning, and relevance because a connection is discerned between skills and content that transcends curriculum lines. In a synergistic classroom, simultaneous teaching of concepts and skills without regard to curriculum areas would have a greater effect than the sum of learning skills and concepts in individual subject areas. (Bonds, *et al.,* 1993)

The concept of integrated curriculum can be summarised to mean that the curriculum is not just a series of jumbled subjects but a permutation of subjects intertwined, interactive, and collaborating with one another. The accent shifts from the class room and content oriented learning to more of enquiry, research and project oriented learning. Therefore the mainstay in learning goes beyond textbooks and subject teachers. A conscious effort is made to establish relationship among different concept and subject matter. Units related to a theme are used as principles for arrangement of courses. The time-table becomes more elastic and even the student grouping becomes adaptable based on interest, context and relevance. In fact integrative Curriculum goes beyond the linking of subject areas. It is a planned learning experience which provides the learners with a unified view of commonly held knowledge by a process of learning the models, systems, and structures of culture. It also motivates and develops learners power to perceive new relationships and thus to create new model, systems, and structures. Therefore, it is an educational approach that prepares students for lifelong learning. (Byrne, 1981)

The advantages of integrated learning are endless. Integrated curriculum facilitates the employment of skills. As said earlier, learning is not just being loaded with information and subject matter from books. It is very much the learning of skills which help the students to analyze, evaluate and apply the content and information to real life situations. Integrated learning provides an integrated knowledge groundwork that leads to faster reclamation of essential data. It is a gateway for multiple perspectives that enhance a more integrated knowledge base. Thus integrated curriculum encourages depth, breadth and range in learning and promotes positive attitudes in students. Integrated curriculum breaks the rigidity and monotony of traditional teaching and provides for more quality time for curriculum adventure. (Lipson, *et al.*, 1993)

Richard Maurer (1994), writing about integration in curriculum for high school students lists ten more advantages that are pertinent for us here. It teaches students how to transfer knowledge. It involves the entire community as a

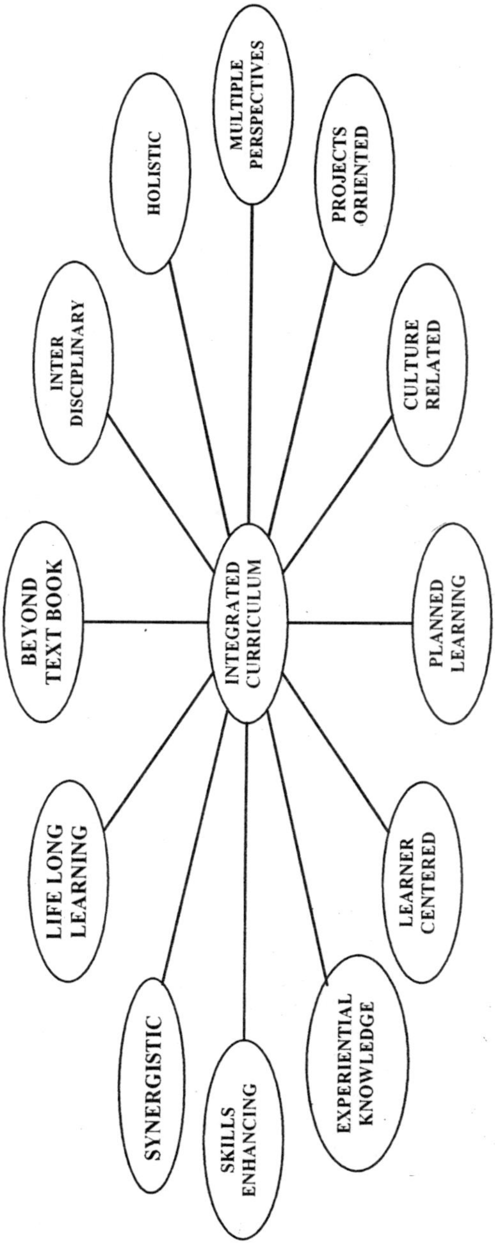
INTEGRATED CURRICULUM
INTER DISCIPLINARY
HOLISTIC
MULTIPLE PERSPECTIVES
PROJECTS ORIENTED
CULTURE RELATED
PLANNED LEARNING
LEARNER CENTERED
EXPERIENTIAL KNOWLEDGE
SKILLS ENHANCING
SYNERGISTIC
LIFE LONG LEARNING
BEYOND TEXT BOOK

learning environment. It teaches students how to analyze, explain, and apply knowledge. It is result oriented. It teaches students how to make decisions. It teaches students how to work cooperatively with others. It encourages individually and diversely. It improves student's retention of knowledge. It provides meaning students experience. In Indian context, it finally eradicates the outrageous habit of 'mugging' up knowledge. It shifts the emphasis from the overrated place bestowed upon 'final' examination to continuous learning. It gives a new direction and life to learning assessment that is genuine and worthwhile.

We can see why it is necessary to move from a conventional paradigm in curriculum design to a new paradigm with an integrated learning basis. In the conventional paradigm, the teaching heavily emphasised content and concept learning. Content learning was priority and one cannot shunt it aside to give room for basic skills learning. Therefore, the traditional curriculum was about important topics and ideas, and instruction aimed to make these ideas come alive. Even the secondary curriculum revolved around traditional content, some times linked across two or more subjects. On the other hand, the new integrated curriculum comprises learning skills and strategies selected based on their values. Learners not only acquire the curriculum content being taught but also develop the capacity to think and learn independently. The integrated curriculum is well planned and structured. It is also defined for all levels: and all teachers, regardless of departmental affiliation. The new curriculum brings integration across subjects, working out a sequence of learning skills that merge with the content order of each subject. (Jabobs 1989).

However there are certain misconceptions that make the shift not easy. There are those who believe that make the shift not easy. There are those who believe students already have these skills. Sometimes educators feel that there is no need to cultivate certain familiar skills, such as everyday decision-making problem solving. After all, these are part of life; why should they require learning. Secondly, there are those who believe that the subject matters already embody these skills. It is often believed that nothing specific need be done about thinking skills. There are also those who say that skills learning require not only time but a certain level of intelligence and comprehension. Not all our students have such abilities. Therefore, they believe and suggest that skills are for the more intelligent and content is for all. (Jabobs, 1989)

Educationists have identified three approaches to curriculum provision and the consequent outcomes. The first one is called the subject content approach. Traditionally all educational institution uses this approach. It concentrates on the courses, subject and content that students learn and master at respective levels. Therefore, the outcomes and assessments are specific to content learning and related skills acquisition. This is done through tests, assignments and examinations at the end of the course. Therefore, the outcomes are short range and specific to a subject area. Most often, it does not relate to what is happening in other areas. This approach is essential where we want our learners gain certain knowledge and skills necessary at that particular level. It would be irrational to do away with this approach. The second is the competencies approach. Besides the content, this approach gives significant values. It is concerned with principles that sustain human compatibility and progress. Learning is not haphazard, whimsical but value-based. Both content and values are viewed critically. The skills of critical thinking become crucial for determining facts and plan of action. It is concerned with problem solving and equips learners accordingly.

Knowledge is not for the sake of knowledge but for making life more enjoyable and for making the world better place for everyone through edification. Therefore, learning does not confine itself to the classroom to a rigid curriculum. It takes seriously all aspects that influence human life and behaviour. It is holistic in content, approach and application. With essential skills in place and with an attitude of openness learning becomes a life long process. The third is the role performance approach. It makes an excellent cohort for competencies approach. Experience plays a key role. It is in the process of doing that learning takes place best. It is in an action oriented approach that moves from theoretical assumptions to application. Truth and knowledge should be demonstrable. Therefore identifying issues and struggling with diversified and controversial situations is the inevitable style of this approach. Its primary thrust is issue-based learning. Learning happens through action-reflection in real world. Hence a, combination of all three approaches with a definite emphasis on the later two will provide an integrated curriculum. (Ackerman and Perkins, 1989)

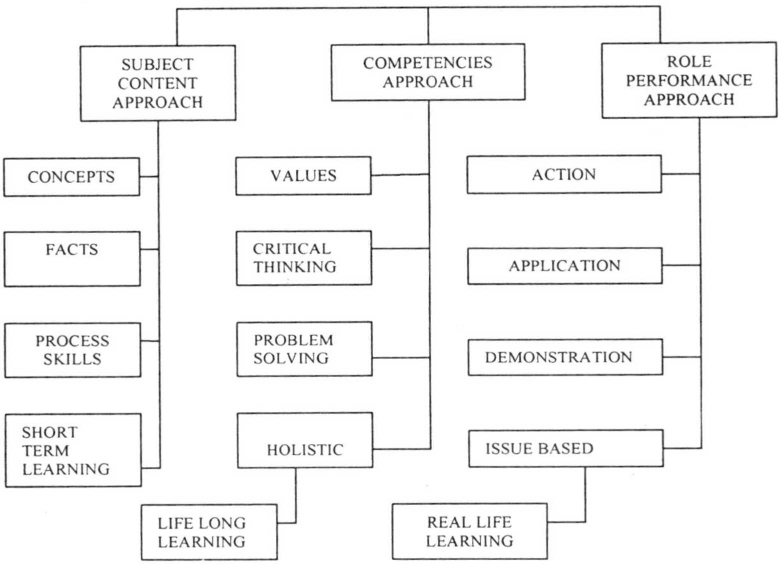

How to Develop an Integrated Curriculum

To begin the process of developing an integrated curriculum we need to ask some basic question: whom will the curriculum serve? What will be the general area of focus? Which subject areas are integrated? (Shoemaker, 1989). The next step is to identify some of the essential components of an integrated curriculum. Firstly, identify core skills and progression. These include basic skills such as reading, languages as well as social skills and problem solving. Secondly, identify curriculum strands and themes. Build the curriculum around these organising principles. Thirdly, then commitment integrate content from multiple areas. Divide each curriculum strand into major themes. Fourthly, the process of identifying themes begins with each team teacher sharing the content and outcomes of a semester course they are currently teaching to the target group. Fifthly, formalise course outcomes. Sixthly, make a selection of meaning-centred activities. Identify inquiry based strategies that contribute to meeting those outcomes. Seventhly, teachers share work sheets and begin to identify common themes or ideas, selecting a theme and sub themes that integrate or ideas, selecting a theme and sub themes that integrate the majority of the content of all courses. Themes and sub themes must be linked to content and process standards identified for the target student group and subject area. Use question to further define major themes and focus activities. Eighthly, to identify unit's development. From the major theme and the questions, knowledge, and skills related to the concepts, teachers plan activities that will lead to development of knowledge and skills that will answer the questions. Ninthly, teachers also collect resources and develop actual lesson plans and assessment strategies, determine student assessment methods and select from possible teaching methods appropriate for achieving the outcomes. Finally, evaluate the unit through an assessment of learner progress. (Shoemaker, 1989).

Activity-oriented and Learner-centred Curriculum

The Choice-Based Credit System works within a semester pattern. In involves freedom of choice, offers opportunities as per-one's skill and pace, and inspires creativity in teaching, learning, and evaluation. It is essentially inter-disciplinary in nature. It could provide scope for application dimension as well as for multi-skill and holistic development, along with an emphasis on value-orientation and social outlook. The credits represent a certain weightage to each curricular and co-curricular components of the course, corresponding to the amount of work desired in the particular exercise. A uniform and simplified credit system should be ideal, without compromising on the essentiality of integrating different components of educational ideals. Its framework should intend to bring uniformity across different streams and at the same time, be simple and comprehensive. (Gregory, 2007)

Efforts should also be on to award due weightage to the co-curricular activities and value education components, especially in the context of growing tendency towards self-centredness, and material tendencies at the cost of social commitment, traditional values and national spirit.

The courses are divided into five parts in all. Part I and 2 correspond to language courses, the former for English, and the latter, with two sub-divisions, one for vernacular and the other for any third language. Part 3 involves the core learning, with four components namely, Basic Courses (BC), Elective Course (EC), Specialised Course (SC) and Applied Course (AC). The credits of BC at the UG level should be equally distributed among the Main and the two allied subjects, with 18 credits each, while the Main is further extended to include the EC, SC and AC. Part 4 is open Course (OC), and part 5 is Co-curricular formation involving four components, namely Value Education (VE), Practical Education (PE), General Course (GC), and Community Service (CS).

Table 1: Course Components and Distribution of Credits

Part Type of Courses	*UG*	*PG*	*M.Phil*
1. Language – English (LE)	10.0		
2A. Language – Vernacular (LY) and LV	6.6		
2B. Language – Optional (LO)	3.3		
3A. Basic Course (DC) and BC	30.0	30.0	33.3
3B. Elective Course (EC)	10.0	20.0	16.7
3C1. Specialized Course (SC)	10.0	15.0	16.7
3C2. Applied Course (AP)	10.0	15.0	33.3
4. Open Course (OC)	10.0	10.0	
5A. Value Education (VE)	3.3	2.5	
5B. Practical Education (PE)	3.3	2.5	
5C. General Course (GC)	1.7	2.5	
5D. Community Service (CS)	1.7	2.5	
Total Credit (No.)	100.0	100.0	100.0
No of Semesters	6	4	2

Thus the present framework insists on the uniformity of the basic approach for all the disciplines irrespective of the science or arts stream as each stream has its own significance in society while the availability of time and the general objectives of learning are uniform for all streams. The foremost advantage of the credit system is the experiencing of the inter-disciplinary approach, which itself depends on one's knowledge about one's own subject, while gaining an indepth theoretical as well as practical knowledge in the opted discipline. The interdisciplinary/integrated approach could even cross the traditional boundaries of natural science or humanities or social sciences. One of the unique features of this frame work is the inclusion of courses especially in part 5 that aims at developing the basic skill, character and personality, and leadership, as well as social aptitude, environmental awareness and value education and self-centredness in the present day global society. The frame work also provides space for exchange programmes'. It also takes note of the need for making the disciplinary-skill sharpened to enhance one's capability either for committee-research or for a relatively secured placement.

Alignment of Course Content with Changing Job Market

In the changing job market scenario, our universities are still languishing with traditional curriculum that is heavily oriented toward hard skills that too, imparted through rote mode. Thus, a substantial section of graduates leaving universities having no ideas of the business environment and its dynamics, and lacking soft skills that are found essential by the business for maintaining better client-business interaction, hence not recruited by the industry. It is, therefore, time for Indian Universities to start teaching soft skills, team work, communications, negotiation, client relationships management, customer services, business awareness, problem-solving and achievement orientation as an independent subject with suitable curriculum offering it for a minimum of two credits, starting from the first semester. (Banga 2007)

It must be taught mainly in the form of role-plays and case studies showcasing team culture, its customs, attitudes and behaviour and other requirements for the success of team play at work places. Instead of teaching stereotype, institutes must teach prototypes. Panel discussions may be arranged with managers who have worked in different parts of the world for global companies, so that insights into practical challenges of working in multi-cultural teams and work places can be provided.

Institutes must also allocate time and grade to students in order to encourage them to undertake social work to better the lives of the less-endowed in the society, so that such interactions will build a right mindset at the right age among the youth for cultivating the concept of 'social inclusiveness', besides eliminating acrimony between the 'haves' and the 'have-nots'. This will also help them in establishing relationships with their future customers with confidence and ease. In all stream of higher education, institutes must place their students on summer internship with business which they are likely to ultimately join, for having a genuine feel about the business environments and get themselves acquainted with business dynamics well before joining them. This single act of the universities/institutes will give a boost to the employability of the graduates.

All these job call for a specific set of tools. Firstly, the curriculum of currently offered courses under economics, mathematics, statistics, english and psychology needs redesigning so as to make the graduates realise their full potential in the new jobs thrown open by the global out sourcing business. Secondly, there is also an immense need to make these programmes more practical besides being analytical in their orientation. Thirdly, students undergoing these programmes must be placed, at least for a month and a half, with summer internship with a mandate to submit a project report, so that they will have a hang of the business environment in which they are likely to work later. This single innovation alone will make students more employable. The courses in which such modification of curriculum thereof are as under: (Rao and Singh, 2006)

Syllabus for Different Courses

As businesses are getting more and more internationalised and sovereign functions are getting redefined, the discipline of economics is gaining critical importance. In tune with this, the proposed curriculum offers a solid foundation in computational mathematics and quantitative techniques that have today become indispensable for a student of economics to explore newer frontiers of research in the fields of industrial, managerial, monetary and international economics. The programme also emphasise on international trade, monetary and fiscal policies, welfare economics and advanced econometrics to enable the student analyse and interpret economic events both national and international.

M.A. Economics

Semester I

1. Micro Economics
2. Macro Economics
3. Political Economy
4. IT Skills
5. Computation Mathematics/Statistics
6. Soft Skills

Semester II

7. Monetary Economics
8. International Economics
9. Economic Development and Growth
10. Economics
11. Welfare Economics
12. Soft Skills

Semester III

13. Advanced Econometrics
14. Globalisation and Indian Economic Environment
15. Managerial Economics
16. Industrial Organisation and Public Policy
17. Environmental Economics

Semester IV

18. Research Methodology

19. Area Specific Elective I
    Paper I
    Paper II
20. Area Specific Elective II
    Paper I
    Paper II

Elective to be chosen from the following:

Financial Economics

- Financial Market
- Managerial Market

International Economics

- Global Economic Environment
- International Financial Management

Economic Policies

- Monetary and Fiscal Policies
- Trade Policies

M.Sc. Mathematics

Today, virtually in every field there is application of mathematics. In the light of this development, the suggested curriculum offers students a thorough grounding in basic mathematics from where they can branch off to newer fields of mathematical application. It shall provide practical training in cryptography, dynamical systems discrete and continuous; Chaos theory and optimisation techniques. The unique feature of the programme is its intensive training in applying mathematical principles to financial modelling, risk management techniques, economic analysis, simulation techniques, neutral networks and actuarial sciences.

Semester I

Advanced Real Analysis

Linear Algebra

Advanced Algebra

Ordinary Differential Equations

IT Skills

Soft Skills

Semester II

Complex Analysis

Topology

Partial Different Equations

Optimisation Techniques

Soft Skills

Semester III

Probability and Statistics

Discrete Mathematics

Neural Networks

Functional Analysis

Elective-I*

Elective-II*

Semester IV

Modeling and Simulation Techniques

Discrete Dynamic Systems

Control Theory

Elective-I*

Elective-II*

Research Methodology

Elective to be chosen from the following area specific papers:

- **Financial Mathematics**
  - Mathematical modeling finance
  - Exchange rate dynamics
- **Cryptography**
  - Information and Security Systems
  - Data and knowledge Extraction

- **Actuarial Mathematics**
    - Mathematical Economics
    - Actuarial Principles and Practice

* Electives with different specification.

M.Sc. Statistics

The programme aims at providing a solid foundation in statistics per se, and from that platform encourages students to branch off into various application; industrial statistics; statistics management; actuarial statistics; bio-Statistics, etc. It also introduces students to the important statistical sources used in business and government decision making, to make students aware of the limitations of such data, and to develop presentation skills. The ultimate aim of the programme is to make the student competent to apply their statistical knowledge in different walks of research, and thereby, widen their employment opportunities.

Semester I

Mathematical Analysis

Theory of Probability

Distribution Theory

Theory of Sampling

IT Skills

Soft Skills

Semester II

Advanced Probability Theory

Theory of Estimation

Parametric Testing and Decision Theory

Multivariate Data Analysis

Linear Statistical Models

Soft Skills

Semester III

Computational Techniques

Sequential and Non-parametric Methods

Time Series Analysis

Stochastic Process

Industrial Statistics

Optimisation Techniques

Semester IV

Elective-I*

- Paper I
- Paper II

Elective-II*

- Paper I
- Paper II

Research Methodology*

SAS

Elective to be chosen from the following area specific papers

A. Actuarial Statistics

Paper I: Probability Models and Life Tables

Paper II: Clinical Mathematics

B. Biostatics

Paper I: Bioassay Techniques

Paper II: Clinical Trials

C. Economic Analysis

Paper I: Economics

Paper II: Statistical Models

D. Programming and Knowledge Discovery

Paper I: JAVA Programming

Paper II: Data Mining

M.A. English

In the context of increasing importance of English under the ongoing winds of globalisation, the programme provides a sound grounding in British Literature, Indian Writing in English, American Literature and Commonwealth Literature, Literary

Theory and Criticism, World Literature in Translation, Translation Theory and Practice and English Language Teaching. The Unique features of the programme are intensive training in Listening and Speaking Skills in English Language Lab., English for Business Communication, Science and Technology, Online Writing and Creative and Media Writing. It finally makes him/her ready to start as an editor or correspondence engaged in content development, learning solutions, documentation, legal services, etc.

Semester I

Language Lab

British Poetry-I (Beginning – 18th Century)

British Drama (Beginning – Present)

British Prose and Fiction-1 (Beginning – 18th Century)

IT Skills

Soft Skills

Semester II

Shakespeare

British Poetry-II (19th Century – Present)

British prose and Fiction-II (19th Century – Present)

American Literature

Commonwealth Literature

Soft Skills

Semester III

Indian Writing-I (Poetry and Prose)

Indian Writing-II (Drama and Fiction)

World Literature in Translation (European and Indian)

English Language Teaching

Literary Theory and Criticism

Journalistic Writing

Semester IV

Research Methodology

Report Writing

Elective-I

- Paper I
- Paper II

Elective-II

- Paper I
- Paper II

Electives to be chosen from the following Areas

A. Business Communication

Paper I: Corporate Communication

Paper II: Technical Writing

B. Writing for Multimedia

Paper I: Online Writing

Paper II: Media Writing

C. Translation and Creative Writing

Paper I: Translation – Theory and Practice

Paper II: Creative Writing

M.A. Psychology

Training may be offered through course work, field work and research in various facets of psychology – psychometrics, counseling, biological and cognitive processes. Once completed, students, as counselors, shall be able to apply the psychological principles in new business organisation such as IT, knowledge management and investment management, to solve stress related problems, besides helping such organisation as professional trainers in toning up of soft skills of employees from time to time.

Semester I

IT Skills

Principles of Psychology

Social Psychology

Quantitative methods

Child and adolescent psychology

Soft Skills

Semester II

Abnormal

Theories of Personality

Psychology of Adulthood and Aging

Biopsychology

Cognitive Psychology

Soft Skills

Semester III

Psychology of Learning and Reading

Psychology of Motivation

Health Psychology

Counseling

Psychological Testing

Psychological Testing - Practical

Semester IV

Research Methodology

Area – Specific Elective I

- Paper I
- Paper II

Area - Specific Elective-II

- Paper I
- Paper II

Electives to be chosen from the following Areas

A. Psychometrics/Assessment and intervention

Paper I: IT and Knowledge Management Industry

Paper II: Education

B. Counseling

Paper I: Family and Marital Counselling

Paper II: Cognitive – Behavioural Counselling

C. Organisational Behaviour

Paper I: Structure and Dynamic of Groups and Organisations

Paper II: Training and Coaching

Such Refocusing of existing programs towards changing job-environment shall not only make these graduates highly employable, but also pave the way for garnering more business for BPOs/KPOs industry which will ultimately sustain the economic growth rate.

Conclusion

There is a strong feeling in the market that growth in BPO/KPO, IT and ITES sectors is likely to be impaired by shortage of workforce with right set of skills and the industries as a whole are looking at the educators to fill this gap. Educators must, therefore strive to build long term relationships with emerging job market segment and offer in conjunction with the well trained graduates with requisite skill sets who are ready to hit the ground running and contribute to the growth of the business. Such innovative initiatives alone sustain our current growth rate of economy.

6

Gandhi on Integrated Education

Gandhian Philosophy

Gandhi was the most dominant personality of the 20th century India. He was the chief architect of India's struggle for freedom. He was not only a powerful political activist but also a prolific writer. He touches all aspects of life and developed blueprints for the future mankind and independent India. Education formed an important component of his writings for more than half a century. Gandhi was no armchair thinker. He put great theories to practice and theorised his own innovative practices. Gandhi was not a system builder, but a theory of education emerges out of his writings and experiments. Gandhian philosophy was based on the supreme value of 'Truth'. Truth occupies a central position in his life and he always gave the highest priority to truth in all walks of his life. He followed the path of truth throughout his life in tune with the Hindu scripture's dictum that truth is the highest duty (Sathyammasti paramodharmah). He lived his entire life for the nation and the society and in search of truth in various aspects of life. For Gandhi truth is the sovereign principle which includes numerous other principles. The truth is not only truthfulness in word but truthfulness in thought and action. The relative truth of our conception but the absolute truth, the eternal principle that is God in his childhood he thought that 'God is Truth' but later he followed the notion that 'Truth is God'. In this way, the truth norm implanted in his thought found its reflections in every aspect of life. It became integral to his thought. He grew more ethical and relative as he relied upon it as a principle of judgment and activity (Cenkner 1989). He applied his idea of truth to social and political aspects at all levels in the later part of his life.

According to Gandhi, every man has right and the capacity to determine truth for him and it is this essential virtue, viz., the ability to determine truth for him, which separates man from brute. Truth rules out prejudice, evasion, secrecy and deception as well as exaggeration, suppression or modification of reality. Truth also implies mutual tolerance and avoidance of dogmatism and bitterness, for truth as discerned by man is always relative and fragmentary (Dhawan, 1990), Gandhi was a great believer in the ancient Indian axiom 'Non violence is the highest law' (Ahimsa Paramo Dharma). Gandhi had always given emphasis on the virtue of *Ahimsa* or no-injury to all living beings. Hindu ethics since the time of the Upanishads has been giving importance to the virtues of Ahimsa. Gandhi also believed in the ancient principle of education; 'Sa vidya Ya Vimuktaye' or education liberates. Self-realisation remained the corner-stone of his educational philosophy and freedom from hunger, fear, exploitation and slavery, etc. were added on. Education for him was not an endeavour for lifelong process. It also included the nationalistic goals. Education is for the body, mind, life and soul. Dignity of labour is emphasised, education must help to bake bread, education must create employability and every student must be equipped with livelihood skills. Ethics was the foundation of education. Education has to be rooted in culture. He was all for a secular and non-sectarian ethics. He believed that to live for others was the essence of all religions. He was not driven by information, not even by limited skills, but by man making. Character building was cardinal to his philosophy of education.

Gandhi on Education

The contribution of Gandhi as an educator and as an essayist in education is indeed manifold. Gandhi enriched and carried forward the century old debate on education. He reiterated the fundamental principle of national education that each nation has to evolve in its own educational ideal based on its cultural heritage, needs and aspirations. Education must inculcate patriotism but no-competitive nationalism. He did not look forward to supplement the English systamic education. He carried forward the debate on education beyond the portals of formal system of graded educational institutions. For him education was a life long process beyond the structured age group of five to twenties. He was for the education of masses, women, adults and the entire country. He did not confine himself to liberation of the soul. He was not for education of a class but for the masses. None before him and none of his contemporaries shouted at the top of their voice for a system of education which would cover all as he did. He was not bounded by any "ism" of education. He drew freely from all sources. On many facets of education.

Gandhi sounds almost post-modern. His support for co-education, sex education, and recognition of place of English in higher education, community involvement for the support of education, universal adult education, universal basic education and opposition to corporal punishment are all part of modern system of education. His concern for the excluded classes and his gender sensitivity were all modern. His recognition of mother tongue as the best medium of instruction has universal acceptance. Similarly, his insistence on respect for labour, ethical and moral characteristic building, livelihood skills are found valid to the present context. And social reforms are as valid today as in yester years. Gandhi was a great believer in the ancient Indian axiom 'Non violence is the highest law'. He also believed in the ancient principle of education that "education liberates". Education for him was not an endeavour for life beyond but it was for life, for livelihood skill and a lifelong process. Education was for the body, mind and soul. (Gopinath, 1990)

Gandhi's Concept of Basic Education

On Basic Education Gandhi has stated,

(a) That free and compulsory education should be provided for seven years on a nationwide scale.

(b) That the medium of instruction should be mother tongue.

(c) The process of education throughout the period should centre around some form of manual and productive work and all other activities to be developed and training to be given should as far as possible be integrally related to the central handicraft, chosen with due regard to the environment of the child that the product of the handicraft should gradually be able to cover the remuneration of the teacher.

(d) Primary Education for children in the age group of 6-14 for both boys and girls, to develop with faculties conducted by school teachers in co-operation with parents and the community. It includes physical nurture, medical care, personal cleanliness and health, community cleanliness and health, self help, social training, development of mathematical sense, craft work like spinning and weaving, nature study, art and music and spiritual development, irrespective of their caste or class.

(e) Secondary Education should be through Vocational Education. The duration is four years, with the same curricular contents for adolescent boys and girls in the age group of 15-18, irrespective of their caste or class. It must provide for a great range of productive activities to support the community and provide the basis for sound and well organised knowledge.

There are some fundamental activities around which the programme of work for pre-primary, primary, secondary and adult education were recommended such as:

(i) Clean and healthy living to focus on personal and social habits and attitudes of health.

(ii) Self-reliance to focus on economic self-support for its own sake and for character building.

(iii) Productive basic crafts to focus on the three most suited crafts for children by age for developing intelligence and general knowledge. The three basic crafts are the main centre of co-relation for the "core subjects" of language, mathematics, general science and social science.

iv) Social service activities in community to focus on developing habits and attitudes of co-operation at home, at school and in the community.

v) Festival and cultural programmes to focus on games,

dance, cultivating good character, cultural awareness, recreation, pleasure along with work, drama, bhajans etc., are relating to social, religious, historical significance so that it enrich their life.

Naturally, to Mahatma Gandhi, education needed to be designed as a tool to attain freedom, particularly freedom for the rural people of India. He could conceive destination as a dynamic force leading to a definite destination. His experiments in education give remarkable views and changes in the minds of the Indians. (Biswas and Deka, 2011)

Gandhi on Value Education

Chakrabarti (1999) explains Gandhi's view on Value Education convincingly from his Educational Philosophy. He says "Gandhiji considers value education as an indispensable part of one's endeavour of identification by means of self enquiry, self analysis and self evaluation. Such type of education for values, therefore, necessitates the approach that harmonises essential components contributing to the growth and development of personality. He warns against the dangers of passivity and dependence on knowledge, which merely turns out to serve but he needs, creativity and critical thinking.

Education needs to be enriched with value. "Education without character" is one of Gandhi's seven major social evils. In various formulations, he presents the goal of education as character building, which focuses on the development of courage, strength, fearlessness, virtue and the ability to engage in selfless work directed at moral and spiritual aims. Gandhi stipulated that education not only moulds the new generation but reflects a society's fundamental assumptions about itself and individuals that compose of. In terms of contemporary fragmentation and alienation and the non traditional philosophical principles of the western philosophy and importance to body, feelings and embodied consciousness, Gandhi's formulation may be instructive. (Swamy, 2010)

True education of the intellect can only come through a proper exercise and training of the bodily organs, e.g., hands, feet, eyes, ears, nose, etc. In other words, an intelligent use of the bodily organs in a child provides the best and quickest way of developing his intellect. But unless the development of the mind and body goes hand in hand with a corresponding awakening of the soul, the former alone would prove to be a poor lopsided affair. By spiritual training he means education of the heart. A proper and all-round development of the mind, therefore, can take place only when it proceeds "pari passu" with education of the physical and spiritual facilities of the child. They constitute an indivisible whole. (Harijan, May 8, 1937). According to this theory, therefore, it should be gross fallacy to suppose that they can be developed piecemeal or independently of one another.

Role of Teachers in Value Based Education

Reorientation of programmes for laying emphasis on values and ethics and quality of higher education, are of major concerns at the present situation. Value Based Education (VBE) is no doubt a big treat to the traditions, morals, ethics, individualism and way of life of students. The technological advancements are not properly integrated with cultural values and ethics resulting in a lopsided generation. There should be equilibrium between the knowledge and skills that science and machinery bring with the values and insights of ethics. Value oriented education is nowadays becoming a well accepted theme in the fields of higher education. VBE is more teacher and environment based than text books or ethical syllabus based. It is more awakening and informing. For this life-oriented education, what we need is to create a special environment in institutions to transform our students for a society enriched with values.

The education policy document by University Grants Commission (UGC), Government of India has laid stress on imparting of value-oriented coaching. It is found that seventy two percent of the science teachers considered it not necessary to impart VBE in the colleges. Twenty eight percent of them wanted the students to be engaged with VBE along with other subjects whether it is science or humanities. Ninety two per cent of the humanities teachers are of the opinion that VBE is essential along with their usual curriculum. But the teachers from both discipline responded that they lacked effective strategies and resources for VBE. Lack of training to teachers in ethics and morality undermines their fervour often leading to the discontent and burnout towards VBE.

According to Amanda (2008) teachers send powerful messages to students through what they do in the classroom and the kinds of discussions they will and will not engage in. For Mahatma Gandhi, "A teacher who establishes rapport with the taught, becomes one with them, learns more from them than he teaches them. He who learns nothing from his disciples is, in my opinion, worthless. Whenever I talk with someone I learn from him. I take from him more than I give him; a true teacher regards himself as a student of his students. If you will teach your pupils with this attitude, you will benefit much from them." (Talk to Khadi Vidayala Students, *Sevak*, 15 February 1942)

Teachers have to self examine values and morals at every level to see that everything they do in the classroom provides an opportunity for the modelling of values. Thus, making an examination of ones own values and how to develop values in others enables the teachers to be influential agents to transform their students, thereby making the VBE a success.

Education that Integrates

Mahatma Gandhi was a great revolutionary and constructive genius. By applying eternal values of life at social and national level in the modern world, he showed a new way to solve the world issue of the present time. He had showed seeds of world-wide ideological revolution in his book 'Hind Swaraj'. It was Gandhiji's originality that he tried out every idea in his own life first and became sure of its relevance and then he applied the same idea on a wider scale. For him individual has a divine origin and a divine destiny, therefore individual cemented his perfection in a spiritual society based on the principle of non-violence, truth and justice. Gandhi recommended that education through useful craft should fulfill the basic needs of life giving importance to manual activities in the system of education .This new idea of education was sponsored by him collectively known as 'Basic Education' and this education was not only holistic and political but also highly decentralised and integrated.

At that time, British Education System was like an 'instrument' through which they sought to maintain and strengthen their domination by experimenting with education through implementing a foreign language. This system had inadequate facilities for children as well as poor enrolment, no facility for women education and disorganised villagers, made them helpless and paralysed their thinking and sunk them into poverty and unemployment. Gandhiji viewed all these ill effects of the education system and gave a solution as the form of basic education through which economic, political and social upliftment can be possible. It was Gandhi, who in 1937 first recognised the basic education plan based on his wisdom and successful experiment on education in South Africa later in his Ashram School at India. The vital objective of his model was to develop productive and social skills among the masses. Education according to Mahatma Gandhi was not expression but a modified method to suit the goal of nation building of the new India. He was thinking of revolutionary type of education for upliftment of the vast rural India, a prime goal and for this, National Education Conference was held at Wardha, where a committee of distinguished educationist headed by Dr. Zakir Hussain was entrusted with planning syllabus for the basic education. The report of the Committee along with the detailed syllabus was published in 1938.

Researches Conducted on the Educational Philosophy of Mahatma Gandhi–A Brief Review

Gandhiji's contribution consisted in his philosophy and the social outlook he sought to develop through craft and the mental temper he wished to indicate. He made craft work the pivot of his educational system, as he made "charka" the symbol of the national struggle for independence. The central purpose of Ghandhian scheme of education was character building. Another important feature of his scheme might be noted in the direction of the productive work which was given its rightful place in the child's life.

Siddiqi, (1971) has studied "Mahatma Gandhi's conception of socialism with special reference to its bearing on education and politics". In this study he finds that Ghandhiji's whole philosophy was woven round 'man'. By democracy, he meant the fullest play of individuality. He conceived of a classless, stateless society where everyone is a full bloom human. The whole socialistic concept is based on the community unity and non-violence, segregation of whites and high class Hindus. The political power, according to Gandhi is not an end in itself but a means to help people to better their lives. The whole society will be family of individuals and the relation will be the relation of interdependence. He stood for the education of the masses so that everyone could come up to his fullest potentiality. His thought on socialism, state and its impact took shape in the scheme of basic education. He found that the country became poor and week and under the foreign domination where the Indian culture and ideals tended to be neglected and hence, on the basis of the observation Basic Education Scheme was put forward with a detailed note on aims of education, methods of instruction and curriculum.

Sen. (1973) has studied "Mahatma Gandhi's Educational Philosophy". The objective of the study was to ascertain the place of Gandhiji as an eminent educational philosopher. The study has adopted a historical cum critical method. The study is based on a society free from exploitation. The idea behind basic education is that the handicraft is one of the media of learning. Productive labour should be carried out in an atmosphere of freedom and love. Many students from basic education have found employment in Khadi Gramodyog Commission and social services institutions. There is ample opportunity for the development of mind, body and spirit of the individual in basic education. Women with necessary qualities may be preferred as teachers for primary schools.

Gigoo, (1976) has studied, "Gandhian Educational Philosophy and World Peace." His study had the following aims:

- to interpret Gandhian philosophy in term of education
- to find out the practicability of the Ghandian Educational Philosophy in educational institutes
- to interpret the practical usability of the Gandhian Educational Philosophy.

In terms of teaching in the educational institutions for establishment of peace in the world, the study revealed the following: Gandhian educational philosophy in schools and colleges could result in all round development of students by bringing down the serious gaps in their wholesome development. It gives a spiritual development, teachers and students to further their physical, intellectual and spiritual needs. Gandhian educational philosophy stresses on 'service to humanity' irrespective of caste, creed, colours, religion or nation. It emphasises the promotion of everlasting world peace. It emphasises spiritual unity which is based on a social order. This new social order will help to bring down the gulf between 'haves" and 'have-nots', by laying stress on equal distribution of wealth and necessities of life. It enlightens the ignorance of worldly people with supreme spiritual orderliness in this universe, According to Gandhi 'Truth is God', 'Truth is End' and non-violence is the means to achieve the goal (God). The ultimate aim of Gandhian Educational Philosophy is 'self-realisation'. According to Gandhian Educational Philosophy peace can be established through true religion, human interaction, science, Nai-Talim, socialistic democracy and non-violence.

Dev, (1981) has studied, "The Spiritual Element in the Educational Philosophy of Mahatma Gandhi". The study was:

- to investigate the spiritual foundation of the activities of Gandhi
- to prove that the actual purpose of all education was self-realisation, a purpose which was impossible to attain without Sadhana or spiritual discipline.
- to show what extent the spiritual foundation of Gandhi's philosophy of life and education was both important and relevant to the purpose of education.

Relevant information was procured through library studies, consultation and with the use of questionnaire. The major findings of this study were: Gandhiji's life was mostly an effort in spiritual growth to arrive at self-realisation as well as God realisation, which is called the 'Truth'. Considering this as the goal, the means he used were love and non-violence and all taken according to him was 'a religion of service, through which he wanted to establish a moral and spiritual order in the world society'. To help the child to be successful in life the teacher who is the guide, must see to it that the child is motivated and he as a teacher is doing his work properly with love, self respect, dignity as well as respect and consideration for others. Gandhiji wanted man to be proficient, efficient and productive by knowing himself and his environment. Then only the person would see the possibility of spiritual growth within himself.

Mahatma Gandhi's ideas are based on truth, non-violence and for the socio-economic development and cultural reconstruction, all-round harmonious development, constructive and productive manual labour, taken on a community basis and practiced as his educational principle. Philosophy of education of both Mahatma Gandhi and Rabindranath Tagore are found to be similar in the broader perspective. Both of them perceive education as the tool for overall development and manifestation of man. To make universal man or a complete man was the aim of integrated education propagated by Gandhi and Tagore.

7

Tagore on Integrated Education

Tagore as an Educationist

Rabindranath Tagore (1861-1941), the Nobel laureate, was a great Indian thinker. Though he had no institutional education his contribution to education is incredible. Santhinketan (the abode of peace) is a living memory for his greatness. He had not propounded any new philosophical system and yet had a great understanding of life and man. His ideal of education is consistent with the ideals of life. "It is the duty of any human being to master, at least to some extent, not only the language of intellect, but also that personality which is language of art. It is a great world of reality for man, vast and profound, leading to creative nature. This is the world of Art". Hence he says "......the vision of the infinite is in all forms of creation, in human relationship of love to feel it in the air we breathe, in the earth on which we live and die." As in education so in life Tagore had sought bliss. He writes "The highest mission of education is to help us realise the inner principle of unity of knowledge and all the activities of our social and spiritual being." Thus, for Tagore, true education meant the realisation of unity and harmony of the human life with all existence. Tagore sees education as the harmonisation of human nature with universal nature. In other words Tagore views education as the process of evolving new patterns of life culminating in the realisation of universal man. (Pani 1986)

Tagore was an educationist, scholar, freedom fighter, writer and painter. His contribution to Indian literature and to education system was immense. He won the Nobel prizes in 1913 for his collection of poems 'Gitanjali'. Tagore gave a dynamic open model of education in his school at Santiniketan. He dedicated forty years of his life to this institution. Tagore's schools contained a school as well as a university known as Viswa-Bharathi and rural education centre known as Sriniketan. Tagore's model of education is a well experimented one. The aim of his education model was harmonious development of the individual. It helps to generate self employment opportunities, develop proper value system, which can eradicate social evils like dishonesty, corruption and terrorism. Tagore's version on education was deeply rooted in one's immediate surroundings but connected to the cultures of the wider world, predicated upon pleasurable learning and individualise to the personality of the child. In Tagore's view education was not only for intellectual development but also development of aesthetic nature and creativity. The quest for knowledge and physical activity in one's own agreeable environment were integral parts of the process.

Freedom and creativity are linked in Tagore's thought, one conditioning the other. He was against English language as the medium of instruction. He felt that use of English in education hindered assimilation of what was an additional burden for young Indian students. Hence, he emphasised on the use of mother tongue as the medium of instruction. His philosophy of education also mentions that equal free educational opportunities for all. He felt that curriculum should orbit organically around nature with classes held in the open air under the trees to provide spontaneous knowledge from the plants and animal kingdom. Gandhi was inspired by Tagore's scheme of teaching through 'craft' education. According to Tagore, education was the great liberating force to which all others were subordinate and can change the individual's mentality. The prosperity of a country depends upon the education of the masses and the prosperity will be lasting to the extent which its education is deep and lasting. National unity of a country depends upon its cultural unity which is imparted by education alone. It is education which is the means to bridge the difference between the higher classes and the masses and the gulf existing among the different groups of people in the country. For Tagore, education is the vehicle of progress and it had power to mould the society. He knew that the villages have been the mother of civilisation, especially in agricultural countries like India. Hence, he gave the top priority for the rural reconstruction and upliftment of village people so that they enjoy their life and can develop the spirit of self determination and self-reliance. (O'Connell, 2002)

Education Principles and Teachings of Tagore

Aims of Education

Harmony with Natures

According to Tagore, the highest aim of education is that which does not merely give us information but keeps our life in harmony with all existence. Tagore laments that from our very childhood, habits are formed and knowledge is imparted in such a manner that our life is weaved away from nature and our mind and the world are set in opposite of our days. We rob the child of his earth to teach geography, of language to teach him grammar. His hunger is for the Epics, but he is supplied with chronicles of facts and dates:

- Education should develop a creative mind.
- Education should aim at developing aesthetic sense.
- Education should prepare an individual for a vocation.
- Education should develop international understanding.
- Education should develop values of simple living.

Role of Teacher

"I have found that little children learn more quickly the attitude of the teacher than the knowledge imparted by him."

"Most teachers do not know that in order to teach the boys they have to be boys, unfortunately school masters are obsessed with the consciousness of their dignity as grown up persons and as learned men and therefore they always try to burden the children with their grown up manners and their manners and that hurts the mind of the students unnecessarily."

"A teacher can never truly teach unless he is still learning himself. A lamp can never light another lamp unless it continues to burn its own flame. The teacher who has come to the end of his subject who has no living traffic with his knowledge, but merely repeats his lessons to his students can only load their minds, he cannot quicken them."

Curriculum

Tagore recommended a curriculum for the full man satisfying the spiritual, the creative, the aesthetic and the vocational aims of education. In his experimental school at Santiniketan, science (especially the experimental science) was taught to children in various classes. Natural Study was taught right in the midst of nature, Education values of crafts, projects, music, dancing, fine arts, etc. were taught in his school.

Methods of Teaching

Tagore strongly criticised the bookish and examination oriented teaching. He stressed movement of the whole body in various learning activities. He followed the activity principle, and advocated constructive and creative activities. He believed that there should be daily practice by the pupils in expressing immediately that they are learning. "Work should be wedded to joy". Tagore also emphasised the principle of curiosity and interest, and the spirit of play. He advocated fullness of experience: physical, mental, aesthetic and emotional.

Religious Education

Tagore stressed religious education through practice:

"Teaching of religion can never be imparted in the form of lessons; it is where there is religion in living where life is simple".

"Real training consists not in foisting moral teachings built in making religion and morality an integral part of life."

Santiniketan and Sriniketan: Tagore's Educational Experiments

Rabindranath Tagore's father Maharshi Devendranath Tagore had founded an Ashram and a Mandir at Bolpur and named it Santiniketan, meaning 'the abode of peace'. It became a place of pilgrimage where people seeking peace and speculation came and stayed away from the hubbub of life for self-realisation. Tagore thought this place to be an ideal one to start a school and opened Brahmacharya vidhyalaya. It runs on the lines of 'Tapovan' to hermitage of ancient India. He said, 'an ideal school must be an Ashram in which men have gathered for the highest ideals of life, in peace of nature, where life is not merely meditative, but fully awake in its activities where the young and the old, the teacher and the student, sit around the same table to partake their daily food of their eternal life'.

Tagore started his experiment in education in his family estate at Silaidah in Nadia District in Bengal for village upliftment and social work. But he left Silaidah on some serious circumstances and moved to Santineketan and started an Ashram school with a few pupils. The establishment of Santiniketan was a great land mark in Tagore's career as an educationist. He gave gradually a new name to his Santhiniketan School called 'Vishva-Bharathi' with a new motto. "Yatra Visvam bhavatyekanidam" meaning where the world makes its home in a single nest".

Srineketan also called as 'Institute of Rural Reconstruction' was established in 1920. The long cherished dream of Tagore about rural reconstruction was on its way to fulfillment through the initiative of an Englishman and the financial assistance of an American. Sriniketan was undoubtedly launched in its career under very promising circumstances. Agricultural research, education, health, social life in the villages, handicraft and experiments were under taken at .Sriniketan. Sriniketan aimed at combining work with joy, picnics, excursion, games, and music, theatrical performances and celebrating socio-religious festivals constituted regular features to bring students and villagers at work together. The entire programme in Sriniketan rural upliftment was adopted by India's Five Year Plans as a model for rural community developments.

The main objectives of these institutions were to bring back life in its completeness into the villages making them self-reliant and self-respectful, acquired with the cultural traditions of their own country, and competent to make an efficient use of the modern resources for the improvement of their physical, intellectual and economic condition.

The Purpose of establishing Santiniketan and Sriniketan were:

- to teach different cultures of the East, especially those that originated in India or found shelter within her shoes.
- to establish the institute of rural reconstruction in order to lay the foundation of a happy and contented human life in villages.
- to seek to establish a living relationship between the East and the West, to promote inter-cultural and inter-racial amity and understanding and fulfill the highest mission of the present age of the unification of mankind.

Tagore's educational ideals were of harmony with nature, the ideal harmony between the different subjects, the ideal of inner development, the development of all aspect of the personality of the child, with a proper emphasis on the emotions, or intellect, on violation, these are now practically common place in the educational parlance of the world. A model for integrated education.

Characteristics of Santiniketan/Visvabharati:

- It should give spiritual training
- It should help the children for the cultivation of love of nature and sympathy with all living creatures
- It should impart knowledge through mother tongue
- It should educate children by providing an atmosphere of freedom
- It should educate children by providing an environment of living aspiration, based upon living contact between the teacher and the taught
- It should provide an environment after the fashion of ancient 'Tapovanas' forest schools about which he had read so much in the Upanishads
- It should be a community school where there is no distinction of caste and creed
- It should teach crafts like sewing, book-buiding, weaving, carpentry, etc.

- It should include drawing, art and music as an integral part of the curriculum
- It should provide students adequate opportunities for choosing their hobbies and occupation
- It should be a self governing institution which has a dairy farm, post office, hospital and workshop, students hold their own courts
- It should provide for close personal contact with the teacher
- There should be a well equipped library
- The school should provide for manual labour
- The school should be situated in natural surroundings

Training in the use of limbs, development of spirit of questioning, thinking and observation, cultivation of interest and enjoyment in trees, birds, the beast and the varied phenomena of nature, experience in the making of articles of daily use, habit of keeping one's living room and surroundings clean, healthy and beautiful, practice of cleanliness extending to the body, dress and personal behaviour through adequate observation of both, wholesome discipline in eating, physical exercise and rest and careful maintenance of bodily and mental strength. These are essential to the life of this Ashram.

Visva-Bharati or World Culture

The word Visvabharati is composed of two words. In Sanskrit, the word 'Visva' means 'world' and 'Bharati' means 'culture'. The motto of this university is "Yatra Visvam Bhavati Ekamidam", i.e., "Where the world meets in one place". In order to "Establish a relationship between the East and the West, to promote inter-cultural and inter-social amity and understanding and fulfill the highest mission of the present age and the unification of the mind."

Tagore has observed, "I have formed the nucleus of an international university as one of the best means of promoting natural understanding between the East and the West." It was intended to be "Treasure of Light" not only for India but also for the world.

Main features of Visvabharati

1. The institution that bore the name of Visvabharati was founded with the call that man had to be set free not only in the field of nature but also among mankind.
2. The greatest distribution of our school is the direct and immediate emotional contact of pupils with their teachers and with external nature.
3. A speciality of our institution is that it wants to bring up our pupils in inseparable association with nature.
4. It wants to add before the world the ideal of the universality of man.
5. It is intended not only to be the intellectual centre of the intellectual life of India but also the centre of her economic life.
6. It is envisaged to be the nucleus of an international university and as one of the means of promoting natural understanding between the East and the West.

Tagore's philosophy of Life

Humanism: "He (God) is there where the tiller is tilling the hard ground and where the path maker is breaking the stone."

Naturalism: Tagore loved nature.

"He lives in a prison house whose walls are alien to him."

Spiritualism: "I believe in the spiritual writing of man and therefore I ask you to accept this task for me."

Individualism: Tagore believed that every being has the right to shape his life in his own way.

Universalism: "Before we are in a position to stand a comparison with the other cultures of the world to truly co-operate with them, we must base our own culture on a synthesis of all the different Internationalism."

Education and Human Values: Vision of Tagore

Tagore rejected in his boyhood the system of education established by the British rulers, against the system in many of his writings this repulsion was not against English language or English knowledge as such. Infact his mind was wide as acquainted with modern schools of philosophy, science and technology, etc., What he thoroughly rejected was education that was dull, mechanical, bookish, based on cramming, dominating examination, lifeless, joyless and useless. In "Tota Kahini" (The Parrot Story), Tagore described how the bird (Read Child) with its spontaneity, curiosity, liveliness, freedom and joy of self expression was killed by being stuffed with irrelevant information into the brain in the name of education in the school, portrayed as the cage of the bird.

Instead the "Tapovan" idea of education in ancient India was applied then to the present day needs of the country. His idea was to form an Indian identity by establishing a link with the forgotten past that was glorious. He did not resist the positive contributious of the western culture. He emphasised on strengthening our own culture in order to assimilate the western culture and knowledge to make use of it more fruitfully.

The fundamental values to be cultivated in the education system have been very powerful as described by him in the song sung by his students during the convocation ceremony. "Mora Satyer pare Mon Aji koribo Samarpan". "We shall dedicate ourselves to the pursuit of truth; we shall not involve ourselves in speaking, thinking or doing anything related to falsity. We shall dedicate ourselves to goodness and shall not speak, think or do evil things. These we shall do at the risk of purity, distress, punishment and even death. We shall remain happy and joyful in all adverse situations of life including sorrows, calamities and humiliation. We shall accept fearlessly the challenges of poverty, distress, and death, because we have taken the name of Brahma who is the fear of all fears".

The consciousness of our personal relationships with the infinite, it is the true centre of gravity of our life. This we can attain during our childhood by living in a place where truth of the spiritual world is not observed by a crowd of necessities assuming artificial importance, where life is simple, surrounded by fullness of ample space and pure air and profound peace of the nature, where men live with a perfect faith in the eternal life before them.

Tagore wrote; "Thus gradually, this idea of founding a centre of Indian culture, with which I started, enlarged, the full idea, if Visvabharati now included the thought of a complete meeting of East and the West in a common spiritual stringing for the unity of the human race. This stress was now to be laid on the ideal of humanity itself." He expresses his conviction that a real university should represent the country and the people to which it belong. It was his conviction that centre of higher learning must have entry into the deeper strata of society. He believed that sustenance of a system of education depends on its acceptance by the larger society. Therefore, higher education institution should collect and assimilate from all sources and disseminate among the masses. Like the Mankind as Ganges is known in heaven, is hidden from our sight in the disheveled, inter twisted locks of Shiva, yet she permits her water to come down his divine of forehead and flow on as a common stream in from of the doors of more mortals and never stints her favour but is always pleased to fill our pots and pause to the brain with her sacred water. He contended that modern education should be gracious like her. He says, "The brain is connected throughout all parts of the human body by a network of river. The university will have to play the part of the brain and arrange for a nervous system to broadcast its message throughout the country from one end to the other."

Towards the end of his life, Tagore was becoming more and more aware of the necessity of social accountability and social awareness of the students of higher learning. In an address delivered to students in 1937, 'Chhatra Sambhashan", he emphatically stress the following points:

Developing habit of receiving and expressing learning materials through the medium of mother tongue. He emphasised that the link between the educated elite and the illiterate on semi-literate masses cannot be established except through the medium of mother tongue. His mind was totally open to learn the best elements of european culture, but at the same time, events of the world, especially of the western world, were making him more and more aware that there are many evils in the western civilisation against which strong voice of protest should be raised from students of our universities. They have a vital role to play in this regard.

Students also should try to develop a rational approach towards the grave problems facing the country, e.g. the communal conflict, the castism, starvation, disease and illiteracy. He stated, "Cut through the mist of illusion, acquaint yourself with all the shortcomings, stupidity and shameful ugliness of the country without any exaggeration on a manly way, by means of the bright light of the intellect." As one of the earliest educators to think in terms of the global village, Tagore's educational model has a unique sensitivity and aptness for education within multi-racial, multilingual and multi-cultural situations, amidst conditions that acknowledges economic discrepancy and of political imbalance. (O'Connell, 2002)

The tremendous excitement and cultural richness of his extended family permitted young Rabindranath to absorb and learn subconsciously at his own pace, giving him a dynamic open model of education, which he tried to recreate in his school Santiniketan not surprisingly, he found his outside formal schooling to be inferior and boring and after a brief exposure to several schools, he refused to attend school. The only degrees he ever received were honorary ones bestowed late in life. His experiences at Jorasanko provided him with a lifelong conviction concerning the importance of freedom in education. He also realised in a profound manner the importance of arts for developing empathy and sensitivity, and the necessity for an intimate relationship with one's cultural and natural environment. In participation with the cosmopolitan activities of the family, he came to reject narrowness in general and in particular human beings from human beings. He saw education as a vehicle for appreciating the richest aspect of other cultures, while maintaining one's own culture specificity.

As he wrote: I was brought up in an atmosphere of aspiration, aspiration for the expansion of the human spirit. We in our home sought freedom of power in our language, freedom of imagination in our literature, freedom of soul in our religious creeds, and that of mind in our social environment. Such an opportunity has given me confidence in the power of education which is one with life and only which can give us real freedom, the highest that is claimed for many, his freedom of moral communion in the human world. I try to assert in my words the works that education has its only meaning and object in freedom. Freedom from ignorance about the laws of the universe and freedom from passion and prejudice in our communication with the human world. In my institution I have attempted to create an atmosphere of naturalness in our relationship with strangers and the spirit of hospitality which is the first virtue in men that made civilisation possible. I invite thinkers and scholars from foreign lands to let our boys know how easy it is to realise our common fellowship when we deal with those who are great and that it is the puny who with their petty varieties set up barriers between man and man. (Tagore 1929)

Its well as growing up in a household that was the meeting place for leading artists and intellectuals from India and the West, Tagore had further experience which was unusual for someone of his upbringing. In the 1890's he was put in charge of the families' rural properties in East Bengal. His first experiments in adult education were carried out there as he gradually became aware of the acute material and cultural poverty that permeated the village as well as the great divide between the uneducated rural areas and the city elites. His experience made him determined to do some thing about rural upliftment and later at Santiniketan, students and teachers were involved with literacy training and social work and the promotion of co-operative schemes. As an alternative to the existing forms of education, he started a small school at Santiniketan in 1901 that developed into a university and rural reconstruction centre, where he tried to develop an alternative model of education that stemmed from his own learning experiences.

In an essay entitled "A Poet's School", he emphasises the importance of an empathetic sense of interconnectedness with the surrounding world:

> "We have come to this world to accept it not merely to know it. We may become powerful by knowledge, but we attain fullness by sympathy. The highest education is that which does not merely give us information but makes our life in harmony with all existence. But we find that

> this education of sympathy is not only systematically ignored in schools, but it is severely represses. From our very childhood habits are formed and knowledge is imparted in such a manner that our life weaves away from nature and our mind and the world are set in opposition from the beginning of our days. Thus the greatest of educations for which we came prepared is neglected and we are made to lose our world to find a bagful of information instead. Child nature protest against such calamity with all its power of suffering, subdued at last into silence by punishment." (Tagore, Personality, 1917)

In Tagore's philosophy of education, the aesthetic development of the sense was as important as the intellectual if not more so and music, literature, art, dance and drama were given great prominence in the daily life of the school. Drawing on his home life, he tried to create an atmosphere in which the arts would become instinctive. One of the first areas to be emphasised was music. He writes that in his adolescence a 'Cascade of musical emotion' gushed forth day after day at Jorasanko. "We felt we would try to test everything he writes, and no achievement seemed impossible. We wrote, we sang, we acted, and we poured ourselves out of every side." (Tagore, My Reminiscences 1917)

Tagore never talked or wrote down to the students, but rather involved them with whatever he was writing or composing. He tells how well the students were able to enter into the spirit of the dramas and perform their roles, which required subtle understanding of sympathy without special training. The meeting ground of culture as Tagore envisioned it at Visvabharathi should be a learning centre where conflicting interests are minimised, where individuals work together in a common pursuit of truth and realise that artists in all parts of the world have created forms of beauty, scientists discovered secrets of the universe, philosophers solved the problems of existence, saints made the truth of the spiritual world organic in their own lives, not merely for some particular race to which they belonged, but for all mankind. (Tagore 1922)

To encourage mutuality, Tagore invited artists and scholars from other parts of India and the world to live together at

Santiniketan on a daily basis to share their cultures with Visvabharati. The constitution designated Visvabharati as an Indian, Eastern and Global Cultural Centre, whose goals were:

1. to study the mind of man in its realisation of different aspects of truth from diverse points of view.
2. to bring into more intimate, relation with one another through patient study and research. The different cultures of the East on the basis of their underlying unity.
3. to approach the West from the stand point of such a unity of the life and thought of Asia.
4. to seek to realise in a common fellowship of study the meeting of East and West and thus ultimately to strengthen the fundamental conditions of world peace through communication of ideas between the two hemispheres.
5. and with such ideals in view to provide at Santiniketan a centre of culture where research into the study of the religion, literature, history, science and art of Hindu, Buddhist, Jain, Zoroastrian. Islamic, Sikh, Christian and other civilisations may be pursued along with the culture of the West, with that simplicity of externals which is necessary for true spiritual realisation, in amity, good-fellowship and co-operation between the thinkers and scholars of both eastern and western countries, free from all antagonisms of race, nationality, creed, caste and in the name of the one supreme being who is Shantam, Shivam, Advaitam.

In term of curriculum, he advocated a different emphasis in teaching. Rather than studying national cultures for the wars won and cultural dominance imposed, he advocated a teaching system that analysed history and culture for the progress that had been made in breaking down social and religious barriers. Such an approach emphasised the innovation that has been made in integrating individuals of diverse backgrounds into a larger framework, and in devising the economic policies which emphasised social justice and narrowed the gap between rich and poor.

His vision of culture was not a static one, but one that advocates new cultural fusions and he fought for a world where multiple voices were encouraged to interact with one another and to reconcile differences within an over riding commitment to peace and mutual interconnectedness. His generous personality and his striving to break down barriers of all sorts give us a model for the way multiculturalism can exist within a single human personality and the type of individual which the educational process should be aspiring towards.

Tagore's educational efforts were ground breaking in many areas. He was one of the first in India to argue for a human educational system that was in touch with the environment and aimed at overall development of the personality. Santhiniketan became a model of vernacular instruction and the development of Bengali text books, as well. It offered one of the earliest co-educational programmes in South Asia. The establishment of Visvabharati and Santinikethan led to pioneering efforts in many directions, including models for distinctively Indian higher education and mass education as well as pan-Asia and global cultural exchanges. Tagore lay his efforts and achievements as part of a global network of pioneering educationists, such as Rousseau, Pestalozzi, Froebel, Montessori and Dewey and in the contemporary context, Malcolm Knowles who have striven to create non-authoritarian learning systems appropriate to their respective surroundings.

The influences of mental and physical growth with his school Santiniketan were later built. In his own theories on teaching children, which he expounds in the essay a Poet's School, he asserts:

"Do not be preoccupied with method. Leave your instincts to guide you to life. Children differ from one another. One must learn to know them to navigate among them as one navigates among reefs to explore the geography of their minds a mysterious instinct, sympathetic to life, is the best of all guides." (*Social Thinking* 153)

It would allow all our boys and girls during class to jump up, even to climb a tree. This is really why my classes were preferred, not because I was any special good as a teacher." (*Pioneer* 105)

Tagore's educational theories evolved out of an attempt to grapple with issues, first on an individual, then on a local and finally on an international basis. Tagore's initiatives and educational goals in the establishment of his school were, on a philosophical level to free the mind, also on a practical, straight forward level, to protest to the existing system of education in India at the time about Santiniketan "Abode of Peace" he wrote. "It has to be just like our ancient forest monastries, where teacher and pupils lived together in an ordered discipline without the least trace of "luxury" (Lute and Plough 123). According to him creativity, freedom, and cultural awareness were ignored in the local education system. The educational process also divided Indians into two classes, those who received this education and those who did not. The latter was almost completely cut off from the educated, English speaking urban population. He viewed the use of English in education as a primary obstacle and asserted that Bengali must be taught in order to benefit the vast rural masses. His goal was not economic restructuring, but rather emotional liberation from the British which would lead to political and economical reform." The school must be a laboratory not merely for absorbing knowledge or for producing sheltered hot house growth, but for giving out for adventure in the realm of self-discipline and self-government, of self-expression in the world of spiritual abstraction and human welfare." (*Pioneer* 77)

Researches on the Educational Philosophy of Tagore – A Brief Review

A number of studies were carried out on Gandhi and Tagore, but very few were on the Philosophy of Education of Gandhi and Tagore. The most important and significant studies on their Philosophy of Education have been reviewed below:

Comparative Study of Tagore and Gandhi

Subramanyam, (1958) has studied the "Educational Ideals of Mahatma Gandhi and Rabindranath Tagore a Comparative Study with Relevance to Modern India".

Gandhiji's contribution consisted in the life philosophy, the social outlook he sought to develop through craft and the mental temper he wished to indicate. He made craft work the pivot of his educational system, as he made "charkha" the symbol of the national struggle for independence. The central purpose of Ghandhian scheme of education was character building. Another important feature of his scheme might be noted in the direction of the productive work which was given its rightful place in the child's life. Tagore, on the other hand, had social aims to build up a social structure with raw materials of indigenous culture galvanised with western ideas and to achieve the ideal universal society through education. According to Tagore, the objective of education was to give man the unity of truth and bring one's life in harmony with all existence.

De, (1972) has made a study on "Tagore's contribution to education for international understanding." The study sought to investigate into the contribution of Tagore to education for international understanding in historical perspectives. The study leads to the following perspectives. What Tagore did in Santhiniketan and Viswabharati in a limited way was attempted by the UNESCO after more than two decades in a greater perspective. Significant bridges of understanding can be constructed between man and man only in an atmosphere of faith. Educational activity, through the creation of an atmosphere of mutual understanding and appreciation can help the realisation of a cooperative society. Santiniketan is a bold attempt towards creation of the world peace. Development of personality is not complete through intellectual education only. The emotional, aesthetic and the spiritual aspects of the nature of man must also be cultivated through a planned educational programme. Tagore's emphasis on the development of the aesthetic and spiritual nature of man through his educational scheme is a distinct contribution to the field of education.

Singh (1972) has found Rabindranath Tagore as an educator. The main objective of this research was to study the Educational Philosophy of Tagore. In the study, descriptive method was followed and it was confined to library readings. The main findings of this research were as follows: Rabindranath had given vital importance to the indigenous education in his philosophy of education and had manifested it in his own fashion. He had felt that the inclusion of spiritual consciousness in education was indispensable. The material power alone could not teach a child what was required for his life as an Indian. Tagore further, had given an important place to the economic aspect of education in his philosophy of education. He advocated the educational institutions to keep harmony with the environment of its surroundings.

Paul (1976) has studied "Arts as a Medium of Education in Tagore". The objectives of his study were:

I. to find out the scope of aesthetic in the context of the philosophy of Tagore.

II. to study art as a medium of education as envisaged by Tagore.

III. to study art as a medium of education in Tagore's humanistic conditions.

IV. to study Tagore's philosophy with respect to art as a realisation in itself.

The study was philosophical in the sense that the ideas of Tagore were critically analysed, organised and evaluated with respect to art as a medium of education. The study revealed that:

- education was directly influenced by the growing sensibility of the child as well as adequate appreciation of the best traditions of the cultural heritage.
- the central theme of education was elimination of ego passion of cupidity.
- art and humanity were sides of the same coin of the reality.
- there were two dominant trends in Tagore's educational philosophy. One was creative humanism and other was universalistic humanism.
- Tagore as a natural educator who introduced elements of human love, interpersonal relationship, socio-cultural norms and international ideas through his theory of education called education for the whole man.
- art as a medium of education had been a definite goal and mission of Tagore. Beauty and goodness according to him played a greater role in the creation of cultural norms and conditions which were necessary for realisation of higher and higher objectives.

Singh, (1980) has made a study on, "A Critical Study of Rabindranath Tagore as an Educationist". The study, using the primary and secondary sources of literature on Tagore, critically evaluated his life and works, and then tried to build up his educational philosophy. The analyses of the study were as follows:

The life and works of Tagore

The Philosophical thoughts of Tagore

Tagore's Idealism

Tagore's humanism and internationalism

Tagore's naturalism

Tagore's integration

Tagore's educational philosophy

The impact of Tagore's educational philosophy on the various aspects of education.

Tagore's contribution to education and an evaluation of his educational philosophy.

Purandare, (1982) has made a "Critical Study of Rabindranath Tagore's Educational Philosophy". The objective of the study was to make a critical analysis of the ideological contribution of Rabindranath Tagore to the educational practice in India. The methodology consisted of library study of his writing and his practices. Gurukul system that he advocated was a natural reaction to the mechanical system of education that the British imposed on India. Tagore's general philosophy dealt with the concept about God and Nature. For him God was imminent in all beings, Man was his highest creation. Nature also was the manifestation of God. His views on man originated from his internationalism and his genuine humanism. According to him, aesthetics, the science of beauty was the link between human and the divine. The greatest gift that God has bestowed on man was his consciousness. The main principle of educational philosophy was freedom and harmony with the natural and human surroundings. His naturalism was Indian in spirit. His Santiniketan and Viswabharati introduced music, art, craft, dance, drama and mainly aesthetic approach in the midst of nature. Tagore's aim of education was an all round development or education for fullness. The teacher and the pupils used to sit in the shade in the open. The students enjoyed full freedom. The medium of instruction was the mother tongue. The curriculum should not be only on traditional subjects but also subjects like music and dance which helped to realise the all round development of child. Thus, the noble ideal of 'simple living' and 'high thinking' was successfully attained by him through his experiments. Tagore's view on women's education, freedom and discipline and teachers role in education were also noteworthy.

Periaswamy, (1976) has studied on "Rabindranath Tagore's Philosophy of International Education". The purpose of this dissertation was to investigate Tagore's concept of international education. Through international education, Tagore believed that it would be possible to establish peace and create prosperity among people of all nations. He devoted his life to the theory and practice of international education. Tagore established an international university known as Visvabharati near Calcutta, India. Tagore was consistent in his belief that through international education people would understand one another and appreciate better the common heritage of humanity. His constructive work in the field of education is represented by his international school where the whole world has become a single nest. Tagore worked for one noble cause, the union of all sections of humanity in understanding with sympathy, love and truth. Therefore, the main objective of Tagore' international education is to develop understanding among peoples of all nations. This relationship is essential to achieve the goal of creating a new world with peace and brotherhood. This understanding is necessary not only to common citizens but also to the diplomats who make foreign policies. Without understanding the cultural, social and economic problems of people, policy makers cannot appraise the human dimension of world problems. Tagore followed the great sages of India in drawing wisdom from the Upanishads and in interpreting it in a clear form and meaning. Thus he gave India's own ancient message to the world in a new form that was suited to contemporary issues. The more significant fact is that Tagore formulated an education for citizens of the world. His remarkable educational ideal produced a great synthesis of the educational concepts of the East and the West.

The Education system in India is still inadequate to serve the utilitarian of holistic terms. The unbridled pursuits of modern day and even rising expectations in this high-tech knowledge thirsty world often makes man believe in what one sees the most in print and electronic media corruption, dishonesty and violence in familial, corporate world and national and international politics. Education must prepare a man for a life truly human-with an independent, interdependent, self-sufficient, fearless, mutually co-operating and highly cultured existence with a deep and a sense of social commitment and urge for public welfare. Tagore's special contribution on harmony, the emphasis on balance, the emphasis on all-round development of personality so that no one aspect was submerged, no one aspect was sacrificed to develop any other aspect. Of him beauty must be moral, and morality must be imbibed with the spirit of beauty, and in this way, truth, beauty and goodness which he sought to fuse in his educational ideals. Tagore showed the way to Integrated Education for the formation of a complete man.

8

Whitehead on Integrated Education

Introduction

Whitehead, a renowned mathematician, logician, educator and philosopher, looked critically at western education and what it had accomplished in the 20th century. His challenge is just as relevant to us today as we strive to make education most effective in its various settings. His process of philosophy posits a view of the world as a developing web of interconnection rather than disjointed parts or a static monolith. This dynamic view of the world is directly applicable to learning, particularly to explore integrated forms of education. For Whitehead, the principal enemy in the classroom was inert ideas-static, irrelevant notions that move neither the hearts nor minds of students. He described such ideas as "lead balloons" which had no ability to circulate within the classroom environment. His process of philosophy cried out for conditions in which true learning takes place.

Whitehead's thought on education emphasises process and engagement within a changing world. The technologically advancing world is characterised by change; therefore, any static understanding of the educational system will constantly face road blocks. Likewise, a dynamic, integrated system will find itself adjusting to these changes and interpreting unchanging truths in the instability of our times. His process of philosophy allows us to view the world through its interconnections and to proceed to integrated learning and to equip students with dynamic thinking that will adapt within their life long education. (Evans, 1998)

Whitehead's Philosophy of Education

Whitehead's Philosophy of Education (1861-1947) was built on the concepts of the organism and process thought. He always believed that application of the relation of the whole to the part was central to understanding reality. Relatedness is fundamental. All things depend upon each other. Everything in this world is in some way connected with every other thing in this world. "Nothing is in isolation", everything is a part of a whole. (Evans, 1998)

Whitehead applied this thought to education. He liked to use the term "nature alive" which enabled him to look at both of physical and biological sciences from a unique perspective. (Fan, 2004) In his view, "the students are alive". The body contains both the mental and physical attributes of unified experience. No separation of mind and body in this philosophy, the body includes the mental state. That mental state-the mind, perception, and reasoning is our concern as educators. Students do not present to us isolated minds or bodies but themselves as integrated human beings whose relations in the world are experiences that Whitehead's Philosophy of organism explains. (Evans, 1998)

The idea of integrated education is based on Whitehead's philosophy of organism. It urges us to turn from reductionism and instead, to think of the whole in relation to the parts and the parts in relation to the whole. A student viewed from a process perspective is a student viewed holistically. Teachers do not confront a mind, or a body, or cognation, or affect, but, a totality; learners being their whole being to the situation. (Evans, 1998)

Whitehead's Concept of Integrated Education

The world has become a global village. Indian schools are built to cater to the needs of Indian culture and civilisation. Western schools are built on the needs of Western civilisation. But, now the need is to have global schools to satisfy the needs of the global village. So, communications among different cultures and races are more important than ever before. Our school system should teach our children to know, understand and appreciate other cultures and each other. We are isolated if we do not know, understand and appreciate our neighours around the world. We need this knowledge to understand why they act the way they do, what they believe in, and what they consider to be important. Teachers must become translators of different cultures. A child from any nation of the world may be in their classroom tomorrow, and different cultures are just down the street. We need to teach our children to celebrate diversity and the creative human spirit. (Fan, 2004)

Every country and culture has its own educational system. These individual systems meet the needs of a single culture but are not enough for today's global society. The global society today needs a new educational system, one based on the concept of Integrated Education.

Application of Integrated Education

Whitehead frequently underlines relatedness, connectedness and holism. Even his process of philosophy is the theory and practice of educating human beings and whitehead provides a framework, or conceptual matrix that outlines the interconnection of all living entities offering that very basis for integrating. (Evans.1998) Learning is not segmented or modular, but is seamless. Whitehead's "Aims of Education" epitomises his central theme that education cannot be dissected from practice. His stress on synthesis of knowledge and application contrasts sharply with educational theories which exclusively demand mental exercise. His general philosophical position, which he called, "The Philosophy of Organism", insists upon the ultimate reality of things in relation, changing in time, and arranged in terms of systems of varying complexity, especially among living organism and minds. (Evans, 1998).

As educators engage in reviewing and revising their curriculum, they continually find a disconnect, even incomplete and truncated material for one thing, sciences are seen in one "box" and social studies are seen in another. Once interdisciplinary/integrated connections are made, learners begin to embark on an adventure of learning that will enable them to creatively explore all kinds of inter-relationships, breaking boundaries and building bridges that can revolutionise their experimental learning process. Whitehead's process of philosophy draws from the interaction of learners within a variety of environments, events and relationships to vitalise his philosophy of education.

Whitehead's ideas about creativity process, rhythm, wisdom and knowledge are all extremely challenging to the integrated educator. Particularly fascinating is what he refers to as the rhythm of education, romance, precision and generation are key phrases within the rhythm of education, which appeared in 1992, when Whitehead articulated his educational views in a pamphlet "The Rhythm of Education". (Whitehead, 1992) This rhythm is a sequence of three stages to be included within the learning and teaching process. Whitehead defined the three stages as romance, precision and mastery (or sometimes generalisation or satisfaction). The first stage provides the interest and energy needed to carry through the second if the precision of the second stage is not disconnected violently from the initial interest. It is here that Whitehead takes side with the Platonic thought that "students should be taught in play". The final stage of mastery must include awareness on the student's part that something has been accomplished. By 1929, Whitehead had concluded that three similar stages constitute the life cycle of the organic "actual occasions" which are his elemental units of reality. There is for each occasion a momentary phase of encounter, a displacement, a moment of selective adaptation and then a final completion that makes a passage into "objective immortality" of the completed event as a datum for the future. While he never remarked on the relationship of these two it seems clear that the stages of learning are infact grounded in the more elementary three phase structure of reality. Here again we see Whitehead's thoughts on education to be much more than casual conjecture, but part of a philosophy that shows why practice, if it is to be realistic must take place in a certain way. (Gnanakan, 2007)

To be more specific, romance is the first moment in educational experience. All rich educational experiences begin with an immediate emotional involvement on the part of the learner. The primary acquisition of knowledge involves freshness, enthusiasm and enjoyment of learning. The natural ferment of the living mind leads it to fix on those objects that strike it pre-reflectively as important for the fulfilling of some felt needs on the part of the learner. All early learning experiences are of this kind and curriculum ought to include the spirit of inquiry with which all children are natively endowed. The second stage of precision concerns itself with exactness of formulation rather than merely recognising the relations involved in the romantic phase. Precision is discipline in the various languages and grammars of discrete subject matters, particularly science and technical subjects, including logic and spoken language. It is the scholastic phase with which most students and teachers are familiar within traditional school curriculum.

Whitehead's reference of "Rhythm" there is a free flow from romance to precision. In isolation from the romantic responses of education, precision is not part of music. It can be meaningless, cold and ineffective in the personal development of any learner, particularly a child. An educational system excessively dominated by concerns of precision reverses the myth of genesis. Whitehead stated, "In the Garden of Eden, Adam saw the animals before they see them". (Whitehead, 1967). Generalisations and mastery are the application of romance and precision into the practical ideas and classifications. It is the moment of educational completeness and fruition, in which general ideas or the philosophical outlooks are integrated with the feelings and thoughts of the earlier stages and then prepare the way for fresh experience, signaling a new beginning to. the educational process.

Standards appear to focus on academic performances exclusively. Whitehead was critical of such endeavours. "The justification for university is that it preserves the connection between knowledge and the zest for life, by uniting the young and the old in the imaginative consideration of learning. The university imparts information, but it imparts it imaginatively. At least, this is the function which it should perform for society. A university which fails in this respect has no reason for existence. This atmosphere of excitement arising from imaginative consideration, transfer knowledge. A fact is no longer a bare fact: it is invested with all its possibilities. It is no longer a burden on the memory: it is energising as the poet of our dreams and as the architect of our purpose. (Whitehead, 1967)

Whitehead weaves a theme of aesthetic appreciation into his writings which is one of the most important practical contributions to education. Such an appreciation gives experience its full impact and bring with it a sense of reality which neither abstract classification nor practical manipulation will convey. The impact of this sense of reality adds "energy to our experience" and makes the difference between actively engaged learning and detached, passive encounters. We could compare this aesthetic appreciation must include an element of creativity. The teacher must be a creative artist designing the course and the lecture with imagination. The students should not be treated like containers or expository to be "filled" in the classroom and "emptied" in an examination. In the age of online learning the teacher cannot simply be replaced by a computer, optimum learning will only take place when two or more human beings interact within the realms of their God given creative impulse. The teacher must realise the creativity of his students, who will then allow their own individuality to launch a learning process that will be a lifelong engagement with all that is possible. (Gnanakan, 2007)

Now there is a pressing need for bringing out the aesthetic appreciation of the learner to see a much bigger world than the one in which he lives. Whitehead said "Wisdom is the handling of knowledge, its selection for the determination of the relevant issues, its employment to add value to our immediate experience. This mastery of knowledge which is wisdom is the most intimate freedom obtainable." (Whitehead, 1967) Life is much more than the individual and our education must take on the task of transforming knowledge into wisdom.

Coax the interest by the incitement of pleasurable activity. But without interest there will be no progress. (Whitehead, 1967). Interest gives people the initiative to do things. At best people do things because they are willing and not pushed by others. This is the reason they can concentrate on their doing and can use every ability they have and every opportunity they have found to achieve it. Their creativity grows while they are doing things very actively and on their own initiatively. This is the only way people can develop their creative potential "We must foster the creative initiative towards the maintenance of objective values. We will not obtain the apprehension without the initiative, or the initiative without the apprehension" (Whitehead, 1967)

Aesthetic appreciation is the way for human beings to open themselves to a new and a bigger world and it is also a way for individual and others and it is also a way for individuals to transcend themselves. It is a bridge between an individual and others and the whole society as well. Art and aesthetic appreciation build bridges between subjects and objects, the abstract and the concrete, an individual and others or society. For example, "Children and adults have access to feelings that flow through them from the world and connect them to distant events taking place in space and time. These bodily feelings, a base of all experiences provide concrete ways in which human beings can appreciate the intrinsic values of the world around them." (Whitehead, 1967)

Aesthetic appreciation is not only a bridge between an individual and others, but also a bridge among the different part of human being. Human beings make up of different parts as mind, soul, feeling or emotions and body, etc.; these are also the different powers from the inner life of human beings. These parts want to do different things at the same time because their aims and principles are very different. That makes a human being feel he is split and is no longer a whole person. In fact, this is a tragedy of human beings in modern society that pays too much attention on reason and ignores other parts of a human being as feeling, emotions and spirit. (Fan, 2004), "By way of contrast, the methods of 17th century science replace our concrete experience of the subset with abstract categories that are used to measure the phenomena in question and deny the importance of that experience in understanding the world. Schools and universities emphasis upon this methodology produces an imbalanced education with 'Mind in a Groove'. (Woodhouse, 1995) On the contrary, aesthetic appreciation awakes every ability and every power a human being has toward one goal, not many goals at the same time. Therefore, every part of a human being contributes to be achieving the goals and developing well at the sametime. A whole person can be made only in this way. In this case, aesthetic appreciation is a bridge among the different parts of a human being. (Fan, 2004)

According to Whitehead, "Wisdom is the way in which knowledge is held. It concerns handling of knowledge, its selection for the determination of relevant issues; its employment to add values is our immediate experience. This mastery of knowledge, which is wisdom, is the most intimate freedom obtainable. One cannot be wise without some basis of knowledge, but one may easily acquire knowledge and remain bare of wisdom". "The importance of knowledge lies in the use, in our active mastery of it, that is to say; it lies in wisdom. It all depends on who has the knowledge and what and how he does with it. The whole aim of education is the production of active wisdom. (Whitehead, 1967)

Whitehead states that there are three main rhythmic cycles of human growth. They are romance, precision and generalisation. The first is romance, the joy of discovery and the love of learning that distinguish the young child. It becomes the basis of the other two cycles as precision and generalisation. If the child is not taught in that way, ideas become 'Inert' and knowledge remains 'dead'. As a result, the child fails to understand the relationship between everyday life and what he is taught. (Woodhouse, 1967)

Whitehead says, "Moral education is impossible apart from the habitual vision of greatness. If morality does not have support from the inner parts of human beings as the whole, how can people keep it in their inner life forever? The reason is that human beings have mind or reason, body, will and feeling or emotions or even if his body does not want to, how can he do it? If not only his reason, but also his will and emotions and even body live to do, he can get enough inner strength to achieve it, no matter how hard it will be." (Whitehead, 1967).

Integrating knowledge, will and emotions together, it will become real power that can be translated into real wisdom.

Whitehead emphasised that not only sciences, but also literature and arts are very important in educational system. This is also one of the reasons for Whitehead to criticise modern education because it paid attention to only one part of the educational process and left out other parts of it, leaving them to decay and degenerate. A static value, however serious and important, becomes unendurable by its appalling monotony of endurance. The soul cries aloud for release into change. It suffers the agonies of claustrophobia. The transitions of humour with irreverence, such as play, sleep and above all of art are necessary for it. Art is the arrangement of the environment so as to provide for the soul vivid, but transient, values, human beings require something which absorbs them for a time, something out of routine which they can stare at. Accordingly, the great art is more than transient refreshment. It is something that adds to the permanent richness of the soul's self-attainment. It justifies itself both by its immediate enjoyment, and also by its discipline of the inmost being (Whitehead, 1967)

Whitehead's philosophy of education may prove to give an alternative to the present system of education. The new system may be called Integrated Education, Balanced Education or Interdisciplinary Education. As Whitehead did, aesthetics will and must play a very important role because of its character of integration. To have integrated education, the two concepts, cognitive and aesthetic cannot be in conflict, but must be in a dynamic tension. (Evans, 1998)

We should keep a balance between aesthetics and education of science and technology. That is one of the right mixes of necessary specialisation and equally important generalisation. We can avoid a narrow groove as in modern educational way. Then its fruit is wisdom, because wisdom is achieved from consideration of knowledge, experience, emotions and bodily feelings in a broad context. (Evans, 1998)

Need for Educational Reform and Integrated Education

Modern education has its roots in seventeenth and eighteenth century science and philosophy and had much influence in western society. Not only are we surrounded by technology developed from scientific research, we are also educated, persuaded, and required to adopt and utilise the methods of science to solve social, business and personal problems. The notion, science and technology can solve all problem is well established in western society. (Evans, 1996).

Modern educational system is based on the belief and has focused giving students knowledge and equipping them to find jobs. Development of human creativity and spirituality along with translating knowledge into wisdom has been largely ignored. Thus the principal goal of education is making a whole person was lost and replaced by a system of job training. Students became passive receivers of knowledge. (Fan, 2004).

Whitehead was not satisfied with the modern educational system's stress on specialisation. Although sometimes necessary, "this situation has its dangers". It produces minds in a groove. Each profession makes progress, but it is progress in its own groove. Now to be mentally in a groove is to live in contemplating a given set of abstraction which is adequate for the comprehension of human life. (Whitehead, 1967)

Modern education emphasises separation and difference, much more than integration and harmony. Students are separated into parts rather than being educated as a whole person. Disciplines such as language, mathematics and science are natural parts of each person. Schools offer these different courses for the different facets of the individual, but they have neglected to put the different parts of the student together after having separated them. Individual parts may develop very well, but the development of the whole person is missing. Super-specialisation has resulted in a bifurcation of the sciences versus the arts and humanities. Whitehead believed that this bifurcation was a major tragedy for humanity and harmful to the future of society. The world faces the threat of alienation and separation. Alienation creates a huge obstacle for people, nations and cultures, inhibiting communication. As people become slaves of their own specialised knowledge, other parts of their personalities will be obliterated. As a result, they fail to understand the meaning of life, nor do they understand each other. There is a big gap between learning and life, knowledge and wisdom. This leads to a more critical gap among individuals. (Fan, 2004)

Students are not happy about the system of education. Drop out rates are high mainly because of the classroom atmosphere and the examination system. Examination pressures sometimes lead to suicides. Students spent many sleepless nights because of the education system. Lack of creativity is another problem in this education system. Teachers have stifled creativity in the pursuit of the accumulation of facts, and parents have forced children to spend their entire strength to concentrate on examinations. Present examination system produces huge pressure for the students and result in them becoming like machines. Teachers become machine operators, and the parents are the keepers of the learning machines. The students keep busy doing endless home works. The teachers keep busy giving the students tasks. The students cannot pursue any outside interest or relax. They do not have time to think about what they are learning, how to learn more wisely or why they should be learning, what they are learning. They just receive information from their teachers. As a result, students do not develop creativity. But Whitehead advocates, "an education which does not begin by evoking initiative and end by encouraging it must be wrong. For its whole aim is the production of active wisdom." (Whitehead, 1957)

According to Whitehead, "The fading of ideals is sad evidence of the defeat of human endeavour. Ancient schools of philosophy aspired to impart wisdom, but in the present school of thought our aim is only to teach subjects. The drop from the divine wisdom, which was the goal of the ancients, to textbook knowledge of subjects, which is achieved by the modern, marks an educational failure, sustained through the ages (Whitehead, 1957). In the present system of education, the goal is for students to find a good job. Moral and spiritual education of the youth is neglected.

For Whitehead, spirituality means, "a combination of emotion, physical experience, and intellect that accompanies a search for the unknown as in some aesthetic experience, and appreciation of possibilities of knowing beyond that which is directly perceived". (Evans, 1998) This facet of education has been ignored for years in the modern system. For most educators spiritual education or value education is a waste of time. For them, it is not useful because it does not help students to make money directly. Moral and ethical values may go against the highly mechanical life of the world. Consequently many young people in the society have difficulty in adjusting with the changing world even if they are very smart and knowledgeable. Some of them suffer from emotional problems. Some of them have no goal but to make money. Some of them even commit crimes against others and society. They become misfit to face the challenges of the world.

Integrated Education as an Alternative

Integrated Education is to integrate the different parts of a human being for making a whole person; to integrate the different cultures for creating a culture with global view, to develop the student's creativity so that they can translate the knowledge into real wisdom (Fan, 2004). Creativity cannot be developed without interest. Interest is created through our feelings and experiences. Whitehead said, "There can be no mental development without interest. Interest is the sine qua non for attention and apprehension."

To conclude, whether we call Whitehead's philosophy of education an integrated education or a balance education, aesthetic will and must play a very important role in it because of its character of integration. In Cobb's words, "For Whitehead the purpose of education is primarily aesthetic, that is, in the language of adventures of ideas, it is primarily for increasing strength of beauty……. , the overall focus is clearly on what happens in the interior of life of people." Critics of education system ignore the aesthetic, focusing instead on the cognitive. In a Whiteheadian school, these two concepts, cognitive and aesthetic, cannot be in conflict, but must be in a dynamic tension." (Whitehead, 1967) But only aesthetics cannot save the world of knowledge. We should keep a balance between aesthetics and education of science and technology. That is "one of the right mix of necessary specialisation and equally important in generalisation." (Evans, 1998) We can avoid a narrow groove as in modern educational ways. Then its fruit is wisdom, because "wisdom is achieved from consideration of knowledge, experience, emotions and bodily feeling in a broad context." (Evans, 1998)

9

John Dewey on Integrated Education

Dewey's Educational Philosophy

Dewey (1859 – 1952) was a great American thinker. With him the new world began to influence the educational thinking of mankind. Thinking is the process of passing from doubt to belief. It is not an abrupt transition from natural to rational but it is a recognising and reconstructing experience within the world and space of time. He further held that nothing is eternally stable and change can always be understood in terms of changing time and space. Dewey's theory of knowledge is based on the organic evolution of man's mind that includes aspects of thinking, feeling and willing. Knowledge is not different from mind and ideas are only modes of mind. Knowledge is not prior to action but is product of action. Actions enable learning and knowledge is derived from activity. Knowledge also modifies activities. Prime activities include search for food, shelter and clothing. Dewey recognised the individual and society. Primary root of the educative activity is in the instinctive, impulsive attitude and activities of the child but these powers of habits and interests get activated against the social background. Dewey's concept of man is one of a growing organisms with flexibility and capacity to develop in different directions through modification of innate instincts, impulses and interest. For him education is reorganisation and reconstruction of experience. (Pani and Sathpathy, 2011)

Dewey is lauded as the greatest educational thinker of the 20th century and his experience continues to be much read and discussed not only for insights into education, but also into psychology and philosophy. Dewey's views continue to strongly influence the design of educational approaches such as in outdoor education, adult training, experiential therapies and various other innovations in learning environments. In the 1920's/1930's, John Dewey became famous for pointing out that the authoritarian, strict, pre-set knowledge approach of traditional education was too preoccupied with delivering or transferring knowledge, and not enough with understanding and influencing the students' actual experiences. Dewey was the champion of the philosophy of experiential education, which was also known as progressive education. But, lest we think it was an uncontrolled form of learning, it must be known that he was also critical of a completely free, student-driven educational system believing that students needed to structure their own learning experiences for maximum benefit.

What we have begun today to explore as integrated education was captured by Dewey decades ago. He had a gift for suggesting links and activities that made learning relate to real life. For instance, he suggested:

- maths could be learnt via learning proportions in cooking or figuring out how long it would take to get from one place to another by mule.
- history could be learnt by experiencing how people lived in their geographical background, what the climate was like, how plants and animals grew, were important subjects

It is sad that Indian education following patterns of the western system has moved far away from practical experience with growing tendency towards highly theoretical approaches. Examinations are based on reproducing theoretical concepts rather than applying them in actual life.

Dewey and the Concept of Experiential Education

Experiential education is essentially an educational philosophy first developed in the late nineteenth century and has since been articulated in a variety of fields including cooperative education, internships, outdoor education, organisational development and training, and service-learning.

The problem for teachers and students is how to make meaning out of the experience. In its purest forms, experiential education is inductive, beginning with "raw" experience that is processed through an intentional learning format and transformed into working, useable knowledge.

There is a democratic assumption embedded in experiential education; its logic is intended to be holistic and integrative, based on the process of making meaning out of experience. Dewey suggests that the goal of experiential education is that we learn how to transform experience into knowledge, and use this knowledge for our individual and collective developments. Experiential education differs from much of traditional education in maintaining that knowledge is individually and communally constructed by people as they reflect on the world around them. In short, experiential education replaces the dualisms of experience and knowledge, mind and body with and emphasis on a unifying process of communication.

Experiential education can be understood more concretely by asking what constitutes an experience. Noting that not all experiences are genuinely or equally educative, Dewey argues that educative experiences could be judged by whether or not the individual grew, or would grow, intellectually and morally; the larger community benefited from the learning over the long haul; the situation resulted in conditions leading to further growth, such as arousing curiosity and strengthening initiative, desire, and purpose.

The unifying process that is central to Experiential education can make it difficult to categorise the various types: internships, field experiences, service-learning, cooperative education, and outdoor education. Broadly speaking, the competing motives of skill development, vocational preparation, service, content knowledge, and values or spiritual development are not, in fact, competing. Tension among them is a part of what creates the cognitive dissonance that motivates learning. In other words, experiential education generates a logic that drives student/teacher relationships, priorities, time limits, resource allocation, and decision making process.

Education and Society

To start first with Dewey's understanding of the place of education in society. In ARTICLE I – "What Education Is", he summed up:

> "I believe that the individual who is to be educated is a social individual and that society is an organic union of individuals. If we eliminate the social factor from the child we are left only with an abstraction; if we eliminate the individual factor from society, we are left only with an inert and lifeless mass. Education, therefore, must begin with a psychological insight into the child's capacities, interests, and habits. It must be controlled at every point by reference to these same considerations. These powers, interests, and habits must be continually interpreted – we must know what they mean. They must be translated into terms of their social equivalents – into terms of what they are capable of in the way of social service."

There is a strong integration, for Dewey, between the child and his social setting without which all learning is meaningless. Is real life experience for learning something to be spurned? The questions cannot be answered with vague responses such as "maybe" or "it all depends on ...." One of the primary areas of integration is integration of our training with the real life context itself. So in an overwhelming sense education must be integrated into society.

Education and School

There is an even more powerful integration when we look at Dewey's ARTICLE II – "What the School Is" where he makes a powerful assertion – "I believe that education.... Is a process of living and not a preparation for future living". As Gandhi said, education is life. And this is life here and now, not just preparation for the future.

Committed to the belief that "the school is primarily a social institution", Dewey goes on to state that "much of present education fails because it neglects this fundamental principle of the school as a form of community life". Instead

> (We conceive of) ... the school as a place where certain

> information is to be given, where certain lessons are to be learned, or where certain habits are to be formed. The value of these is conceived as lying largely in the remote future; the child must do these things for the sake of something else he is to do; they are mere preparation. As a result they do not become a part of the life experience of the child and so are not truly educative.

Dewey was also critical of too much of emphasis on the teacher oriented approach believing that under existing conditions far too much of the stimulus and control proceeds from the teacher, and this is because of neglect of the idea of the school as a form of social life. He asserted – "The teacher is not in the school to impose certain ideas or to form certain habits in the child, but is there as a member of the community to select the influences which shall affect the child and to assist him in properly responding to these influences."

Education and Curriculum

Regarding curriculum, Dewey proposed this subject-matter should be as he wrote in "The Subject-Matter of Education" in ARTICLE III. We see very clearly what he meant by experiential learning:

> I believe... that the true centre of correlation on the school subjects is not science, nor literature, nor history, nor geography, but the child's own social activities.
>
> I believe... that education cannot be unified in the study of science, or so-called nature study, because apart from human activity, nature itself is not a unity; nature in itself is number of diverse objects in space and time, and to attempt to make it the centre of work by itself, is to introduce a principle of radiation rather than one of concentration.

Of learning history, he wrote:

> I believe once more that history is of educative value in so far as it presents phases of social life and growth. It must be controlled by reference to social life. When taken simply as history, it is thrown into the distant past and becomes dead and inert. Taken as the record of man's social life and progress it becomes full of meaning. I

> believe, however, that it cannot be so taken excepting as the child is also introduced directly into social life.

Education is learning that should be unified around practical living rather than the stress on theory alone. The body of knowledge we share with students must be correlated or integrated to the learner's real life experience which in effect is a "social experience".

Taking this to its logical concern Dewey saw place for "the so-called expressive or constructive activities as the centre of correlation" which even had place for cooking, sewing, manual training, etc., in the school. For Dewey, these were not extra-curricular or even co-curricular activities. He wrote:

> "I believe that they are not special studies which are to be introduced over and above a lot of others in the way of relaxation or relief, or as additional accomplishments. I believe rather that they represent, as types, fundamental forms of social activity; and that it is possible and desirable that the child's introduction into the more formal subjects of the curriculum be through the medium of these activities".

This calls for us to even change our examination systems to evaluate how much student is learning. The grades we give to students who reproduce what we teach in the classroom are appalling. We should be attempting to encourage our students to apply what we teach to their own contexts and giving better grades for those who have learned the relevance of learning to their contexts rather than in merely capturing the essence of the concepts we teach. Dewey refers to "the elimination of the social element", which has led us to give our students all of the academic facts and figures without looking carefully at their practical relevance. Dewey's approach underlines that learning in real life makes a greater impact than any other form of educational mode.

Teacher and the Taught

One brief note on Dewey's ARTICLE V- The School and Social Progress will help us see the lofty role he assigned for the teacher. Affirming again – "I believe that education is the fundamental method of social progress and reform" he follows this with an elaboration of the truth he affirms:

> I believe... that the teacher is engaged, not simply in the training of individuals, but in the formation of the proper social life.
>
> I believe that every teacher should realise the dignity of his calling; that he is a social servant set apart for the maintenance of proper social order and the securing of the right social growth.

The value of what Dewey states is the role of the teacher as the one who is engaged in "formation" with a "dignity of his calling" as "the prophet". This calls for the teacher to become part of the classroom experience facilitating learning rather than merely transferring from his mind through his notes to the students mind as an end in itself. Dewey was concerned for a societal influence.

Concept of Experience

The philosophy of experiential education, according to Carver (2001), can be traced to Plato and has at its core principles what were developed by John Dewey. This is not to suggest that experiential education programs are always informed by John Dewey's thinking, but rather that at the core of any strong example of experiential education lies the embodiment of what Dewey expressed. Experiential education ties to integrate the life experience of students into the curriculum. Examples of experiential education can be found in a variety of settings, including the following types of programs: wilderness based. adventure, community development, advocacy, art and music, service-learning, study abroad, work internship, and youth development.

However, the belief that all genuine education comes about through experience does not mean that all experiences are genuinely or equally educative. For Dewey, experience and education cannot be equated to each other (EE, 14). Students in traditional schools do have experiences. The trouble is not the absence of experiences, Dewey argues, but their defective and wrong character, wrong and defective forms from the standpoint of connection with further experience. This traditional scheme is, in essence, one of imposition from above and from outside. Dewey says, subject-matter, and methods upon those who are only growing slowly toward maturity (EE,4).

Accordingly, Dewey points out that a coherent theory of experience, affording positive direction to selection and organisation of appropriate educational methods and materials, is required by the attempt to give new direction to the work of schools (EE, 21). The fundamental philosophy of these new schools called "progressive schools" by Dewey is found in the idea that there is an intimate and necessary relation between the process of actual experience and education (EE, 7). A system of education based upon the necessary correction of education with experience must take the environment and other conditions into account. Experience does not go on simply inside a person, Dewey adds (EE, 33-34). It does go on because it influences the formation of desire and purpose. However, this is not the whole of the story. Every genuine experience has an active side which changes in some degree the objective conditions under which we experience.

When we experience something, Dewey states, we act upon it, we do something with it; then we suffer or undergo the consequences (DE, 139). We do something to the thing and then it does something to us in return. The connection of these two phases of experience measures the fruitfulness or value of the experience. Traditional schools, Dewey says that experience is truly experience, only when objective conditions are subordinated to what goes on within the individuals having the experience (EE, 37).

Consequently, to learn from experience is to make a backward and forward connection between what we do to things and what we enjoy or suffer from things in consequence (DE, 140). All principles by themselves are abstract. They become concrete only in the consequences which result from their application, Dewey says (EE, 6).

> An ounce of experience is better than a ton of theory simply because it is only in experience that any theory has vital and verifiable significance. An experience, a very humble experience, is capable of generating and carrying any amount of theory (or intellectual content), but a theory apart from and experience cannot be definitely grasped even as theory. It tends to become a mere verbal formula, a set of catchwords used to render

> thinking, or genuine theorising, unnecessary and impossible (DE, 144).

Having reflected on the concept of experience, a next step is needed. Dewey thinks, as it has been said, that not all experiences are equally educative. What are, then, to assess a relevant and an educative experience? He says that the measure of the value of an experience lies in the perception of relationships or continuities to which it leads up (DE, 140). In "Experience and Education" he deepens into these two concepts, i.e. interaction and continuity.

Continuity and Interaction: The Value of Experience

In Dewey's work, a key idea is that interaction and continuity are two core characteristics of effective teaching and learning through experiences. The interaction characteristic highlights the importance of the dialogue and communication underlying learning; the continuity characteristic emphasises that the individual learner must be viewed as the key design element. In other words, instruction must be designed so that individual learner can effectively build on what he or she knows, and have to provide resources and assistance to learn.

Interaction

One of Dewey's premises is that students experience results from the interaction between them and the environment. This is Dewey's principle of interaction. Factors that affect students experience include those that are internal to the students and those that are "objective" parts of the environment. The students' perceptions of, and reactions to, the objective factors are influenced by their attitudes, beliefs, habits, prior knowledge, and emotions. In this regard, Dewey says that we may group the conditioning influences of the school environment under three heads (HWT, 46): (1) the mental attitudes and habits of the persons with whom the student is in contact; (2) the subjects studied; and (3) current educational aims and ideals. For him, everything the teacher does, as well as the manner in which he or she does it, incites the students to respond in some way or other. For Dewey, interaction assigns equal rights to both factors in experience- objective and internal conditions (EE,39). Any normal experience is interplay of these two sets of conditions. Interaction is going on between individual and objects and other persons. The concepts of situation and of interaction are inseparable from each other. An experience, Dewey goes on (EE,41), "is always what it is because of a transaction taking place between the individual and what, at the time, constitutes his environment". Each individual's experience is, in this way, complex spatially, the result of an exchange between and organism and its environment.

Continuity

The other premise of Dewey's theory is called the principle of continuity. It states that every experience takes up something from those which have gone before and modifies in some way the quality of those which come after (EE,27). Experiences are complex temporally, penetrating one another, earlier ones leaving deposits or residues which influence later ones. Dewey explains that people develop habits of emotional response, perception, appreciation, sensitivity, and attitude.

For Dewey, any experience is miseducative that has the effect of arresting or distorting the growth of further experience. In "Democracy and Education" he points out that "the measure of the value of an experience lies in the perception of relationships or continuities to which it lead up. It includes cognition in the degree in which it is cumulative or amounts to something, or has meaning (DE,140). For him, the principle of continuity, also called the experiential continuum, is involved in every attempt to discriminate between experiences that are worthwhile educationally and those that are not (EE,24).

Interaction and Continuity Taken Together

Taken together, the principle of interaction and the principle of continuity determine, for Dewey, the quality of an educational experience. He describes them, as latitudinal and longitudinal aspects that intercept any situation. Carve, (2001) argues that understanding the quality of a person's experience using this theory requires consideration of how the experience contributes to the development. He clearly says that suggestions-the result of a problematic situation – must be arranged with reference to one another and with reference to the facts on which they depend for proof. Continuity, then, not only is a requirement for the experiences but also for the consequences of them.

Continuity and interaction are in active union with each other. The principle of interaction makes it clear that failure of adaptation of material to needs and capacities of individuals may cause an experience to be non-educative. On the other hand, the principle of continuity in its educational application means, nevertheless, that the future has to be taken into account at every stage of the educational process (EE, 47).

Dewey uses the expression "Collateral learning" (EE, 49) to describe the learning that takes place in addition to what results from explicit teaching. If students get bored in school, for instance, they might learn (via collateral learning) that being in school is unpleasant and lessons are boring. Dewey recognised the importance of considering the effects of collateral learning when assessing the quality of an experience. Hence, the costs and benefits of an experience are intrinsically connected with its long-term consequences and include the effects of collateral as well as directed lessons:

> "Collateral learning in the way of formation of enduring attitudes, of likes and dislikes, may be and often is much more important than the spelling lesson or lesson in geography or history that is learned. For these attitudes are fundamentally what count in the future. The most important attitude that can be formed is that desired to go on learning" (EE, 49).

Dewey wants instructors, not to present already established truths via lecture, but to teach indirectly, to structure classes so that they and their pupils identify genuine problems, use the curriculum to investigate and discover solutions to these problems, and, as a result, establishing connections with course subject matter. To borrow Deweyan terminology, he wants instructors to help students build their own "continuities and interactions" with the curriculum. His strategy is to emphasise continuities between school and non school life as a way of adding emotional intensity and relevance to formal instruction, promoting methods of discovery as opposed to mere training. This is the use of knowledge as opposed to mere acquisition of it. When continuities between student and subject matter are established, students – as in informal instruction – have a stake in the educational situation. They are able to remember what they master of the curriculum because they use and care about it.

What is learned besides content in both formal schooling and informal learning are habits of openness, reflection, and dialogue. Education in the classical sense of "paideia", is nurture and growth of persons as individuals and as citizens. This requires stimulation of intellectual and social capacities through the give and take of communication of ideas. The educational community, like the broader political or social community, calls for deepening and widening of meaning-horizons through shared communication of ideas. As even the partial victory of democracy over authoritarianism depends upon liberating thought so as to create individuals who "think for themselves," so democracy requires a liberal and liberating system of universal education. Universal education cannot exist without free and unprejudiced access to information and ideas. Elitism or intellectual authoritarianism, on the other hand, exists only to the extent that the majority of minds are kept in the dark, while a privileged few are enlightened.

It is important to keep in mind that the key to understanding Dewey on democracy is that he sees it not just as a form of government. It is surely that, but it is simultaneously a way of life, an ethical ideal, and a personal commitment. Specifically, it is a way of life in which individuals are presumed to be self directing and able to pursue their own goals and projects. No society which maintains order through constant supervision and /or coercion can be rightly called democratic. Further, individual benefits and the common good are mutually enhancing in a democracy.

For Dewey, the ideal aim of education is creation of power of self-control (DE, 75). Progressive education, to accomplish its goals, must be based on intelligently directed development of the possibilities inherent in ordinary experience (EE, 113-116). Progressive education can only succeed when certain conditions apply: Primarily, this involves use of sound standards and methods to achieving its goals, which are based on providing the best educational experience possible to create confident, self-controlled, and capable citizens. Experience in this sense, is the means as well as the goal.

John Dewey advocates for a way of teaching and learning one where students are active in their learning and where experiences make sense to them and are useful.

What Dewey proposes is a model of education, one that is democratic and participatory. Experiences, in this sense, are fundamental to understand what Dewey thinks democratic education should be. Since democracy is not just a form of government but a way of life, experiences should be able to prepare students to be self directing and pursue their goals and projects. Even though he was criticised by the development of progressive schools, they were Dewey's answer to the desire of encouraging democratic values among students. Designing these new experiences implies to take into account the two characteristics that Dewey mentioned, i.e. continuity and interaction. Teachers are required to discover how the subject matter is related to past, present and future experiences, having in mind the democratic ideal. On the other hand, teachers are also called for establishing means to make students connect with their environment and history. Deweys education philosophy can be taken as one of the models for Integrated Education.

10

Current Developments in Integrated Research

Introduction to Quality Research

Quality research needs grammar of research. The issues related to research grammar like research design, sampling process, hypothesis, statistical design; bibliography, etc. have to be made clear that the researchers do not remain confused. Current developments in research that exist in the country as well as that of the world should be made clear to researchers. It is important to grasp varied theories of action implied and to analyse assumptions and values in different research designs. It connotes that research process and research problems should be such that these should solve societal problems from different angles. The researcher has to find solutions to these problems. Providing research answers to such problems and giving theoretical base to issues like these will help add quality of research. Solutions to such problems involve knowledge of related disciplines such as sociology, psychology, philosophy, economics, basic sciences, etc. Knowledge of various disciplines will help building an integrated theoretical base for the research design. A workable solution will emerge out of these. A research providing solutions to societal problems is quality research.

At present, the researchers are provided with basic theoretical knowledge of research process at the master level. For their doctoral research they get in touch with the mentor/ supervisor who without putting the researcher to learn the research process directs him/her in selecting a topic for the research. That is why most of the research topics/proposals match to the research thesis of the mentor. Further the pedagogy of research in most of the cases remains up to the counselling of the mentor. There is a need to change this pedagogical process. Institutions will have to take up the challenge by formally introducing inter-scholar and teacher-scholar interactions. Regular seminars in institutions on research need to be initiated where all research scholars and interested faculty should discuss research problems, methodological issues of research, various implications of findings, etc. Each of the sessions should involve in debates and followed by individual feedback performance in the seminars with an open mind. Experts can be invited to participate in the seminars. Outcomes of the deliberations can be taken for publication.

The research institutions should identify their thrust or the areas of specialisation wherein the research issues would be identified. It should be left to the research scholars to state their area of interest and then identify the mentor and institutions where he/she would like to get registered for research. The thrust area of pedagogy will be easily understood by the researcher and reputed institutions will come forward to provide with the necessary manpower thoroughly oriented in research techniques. Further, the concentration of research in certain areas will help in the formation of group of researchers (research circle) who develop into teams pursuing common goals. These teams and the inter-teams, intra-teams interaction will provide major input to bring quality improvement in research. (Malhotra, 2009)

Integrative/Integrated Research

In the development of knowledge two things are happening simultaneously, one micro specialisations; the other, integration and interrelationship between different disciplines. Such a scenario demands creation of institutions focusing not only on specialised fields but providing research in multidisciplinary fields. Knowledge is developing most rapidly at the intersection of disciplines. Integration takes us away from too much specialisation that many times proves to be ineffective. The profile of the learners that will fit into the 21st century, as outlined by Christopher Ball, (2009) whose educational work has placed great importance on the benefits of society giving enough attention and resource, to the developmental needs of the learners has become highly significant. He envisions the future learners to be flexible generalists rather than specialists. The flexible generalists are persons equipped with necessary levels of knowledge, skills and values to adjust readily to multiple career challenges and make through their own personal development a significant contribution to the life of the country and the world at large.

Integrated or Trans-disciplinary Research creates new opportunities for research design to become multi-disciplinary and this, in turn, creates novel possibilities for better interdisciplinary research communication and innovative research outcomes. When one shifts outside the parameters established by accepted research paradigms and academically constructed disciplines one starts to work transdisciplinary. The determinants of a potential solution involve the integration of different skills in a frame work of action. This provides the researcher with the opportunity to be creative, by making use of the methods best suited to get the proper process covered and the results reflected. In the design disciplines this brings together the processes of innovation, visualisation and imagination. Communication plays an important role in integrated research. The communication between the researcher and the community leads to new research configurations and combinations. The key factor in this type of research method used is based on stimulating, initiating and facilitating communication.

It is evident that integrated research requires a new approach to research. With an increasing number of research participants and variety in research topics, single institution systems are unable to accommodate research requests. Instead facilitating a research system, based on centre-to centre research, to accommodate and broaden the scope of interdisciplinary and multidisciplinary research is the need of the day.

Integrated Curriculum

To evolve integrated curricula for different disciplines,

adequately networking with teaching learning and evaluation strategies, based on available infrastructure and human resource factors, socio economic expectations and international norms are involved.

There are five reasons that denote the importance of integrated learning education: Firstly, it integrates learning with real life experience. Secondly, it integrates theories and concepts to real life. Thirdly, it enhances the particular gift of the learner. Fourthly, it integrates several areas of learning hither to barricaded and isolated by knowledge fields and departments. Fifthly instead of being shackled by a well-used method of learning it employs and exploits several methods of educational deliveries. (Ken Gnanakan, 2007)

Curriculum is the point of contact between the intentions, which initiate education reforms and reality of teaching learning encounters, which ultimately determines the success of changes attempted. Evaluation of achievements of instructional objective, namely, knowledge comprehension and application specified through curricula is an integral part of teaching learning process. Minimum standard of instruction regulations, interdisciplinary merger of skill based courses are essential for the growth and development of the students.

Example:

1. The discipline of plant sciences have become more applied, since it is fully integrated with economic and industrial development.
2. In China, Basic Science is revamped through a new modernisation programme of economic development, namely, industry, agricultural sciences, technology and national security/defense.

Higher education should be responsive to the community, whether, regional or local is under considerable discussion at present times. According to Policy Frame for the Development of Education in India, adopted by UGC in 1977, every student be given grounding in four essential areas namely: foundation course, core course, applied course, field activities.

Identification of the Factors for the Curriculum Development

1. **Goals and Objectives:** It should be redefined to bring

out clarity and direction to the faculty and students, so as to make effective transaction of the curricular contents in the classrooms.

2. **Grounding the Core Disciplines:** Fundamentals of the subject as the core of the disciplines.
3. **Curricula:** Curriculum should not be static. It must change always as the frontiers of the knowledge expand with the time
4. **Social Relevance of the Contents:** Following three parameters may be considered: 1. Value frame of reference (including philosophical, cultural and ethical values) 2. Economic development 3. Social transformation.
5. **Students Need and Interest:** As assessed through systematic interaction with the students.
6. **Pedagogical Techniques:** Suitable methodology for teaching, laboratory study and evaluation should be identified, considering the nature of the content points of the syllabus.
7. **International Norms:** The content area of the curricula should be developed in accordance with current status of knowledge, development and trends of researches carried out in India and Abroad.
8. **Integrating Technology and Pedagogy:** Technology integration is emerging in the information era-educators, media, IT professionals, policy makers, planners, researchers and administrators have to work and plan together.
9. **Evaluation Procedure:** A blueprint of the evaluation tool should be designed on the basis of instructional objectives, content area and forms of the questions, time allocation and difficulty level.
10. **Field Testing:** Developmental try out of curricular materials should be planned to test the validity and reliability of the curriculum. (Sam Daniel, 2007)

Model

Indian Institute of Technology (IIT) M.A. Integrated Programme.

A Five Year M.A. programme in IIT-Chennai aims to churn out good research scholars. The students will be exposed to a wide range of discipline including mathematics and technology.

1. Combined study of - Social Sciences
   - Mathematics
   - Technology
   - Foreign language
   - Indian Issues
2. Major – Development Studies/Economics/English

   Minor – Mathematics/Technology/Foreign Language/ Indian Issues

   Electives: Indian Civilisation, Indian Economy, Indian Writers, Ethics,

   Environment, ICT, Rural Development, e-governance.

   Study of a Foreign Language is compulsory.
3. Six months of project work
4. A Semester long dissertation.

II. Design-Based Research Method (DBR)

Design-Based Research (DBR) is a systematic but flexible methodology aimed to improve educational practices through integrative analysis, design, development and implementation, based on collaboration among researchers and practitioners in real-world settings, and leading to contextually-sensitive design principles and theories. (Wang and Hannafin, 2005)

Design-Based Research is a lens or set of analytical techniques that balances the positivist and interpretive paradigms and attempts to bridge theory and practice in education. A blend of empirical educational research with the theory-driven design of learning environments, DBR is an important methodology for understanding how, when, and why educational innovations work in practice. DBR method aims to uncover the relationships between educational theory, designed artifact, and practice. In recent years, educators have been trying to narrow the chasm between research and practice. Part of the challenge is that research that is detached from practice "may not account for the influence of contexts, the emergent and complex nature of outcomes, and the incompleteness of knowledge about which factors are relevant for prediction". (DBRC, 2003)

According to Collins *et al.* (2004), Design-Based Research (also known as design experiments) intends to address several needs and issues central to the study of learning, including the following:

- The need to address theoretical questions about the nature of learning in context.
- The need for approaches to the study of learning phenomena in the real world situations rather than the laboratory
- The need to go beyond narrow measures of learning.
- The need to derive research findings from formative evaluation.

Characteristics of Design-Based Research experiments include:

1. addressing complex problems in real, authentic contexts in collaboration with practitioners.
2. applying and integrating known and hypothetical design principles to render plausible solutions.
3. conducting rigorous and reflective inquiry to test and refine innovative learning environments.
4. intertwined goals of (1) designing learning environments, and (2) developing theories of learning.
5. research and development through continuous cycles of design, enactment, analysis, and redesign.
6. research on designs that must lead to sharable theories that help communicate relevant implications to practitioners and other educational designers.
7. research must account for how designs function in authentic settings.
8. development of such accounts relies on methods that can document and connect processes of enactment to outcomes of interest. (DBRC, 2003)

Design-Based Research vs. Traditional Evaluation

The following excerpt highlights the difference between the goals and contributions of Design-Based Research methods can offer and Traditional evaluation:

> "In traditional evaluation, an intervention (e.g. a textbook, an instructional program, a policy) is measured against a set of standards. During formative evaluation, iterative cycles of development, implementation, and study allow the designer to gather information about how an intervention is or is not succeeding in ways that might lead to better design. Then the intervention is 'frozen', and the rigorous summative evaluation begins. Like formative evaluation, design-based research uses mixed methods to analyse an intervention's outcomes and refine the intervention. Unlike evaluation research, design-based research views a successful innovation as a joint product of the designed intervention and the context. Hence, design-based research goes beyond perfecting a particular product. The intention of design-based research is to inquire more broadly into the nature of learning in a complex system and to refine generative or predictive theories of learning. Models of successful innovation can be generated through such work — models, rather than particular artifacts or programs, are the goal." (DBRC, 2003)

DBR method focuses on designing and exploring the whole range of designed innovations; artifacts as well as less concrete aspects such as activity structures, institutions, scaffolds and curricula. Importantly, DBR goes beyond merely designing and testing particular interventions. Interventions embody specific theoretical claims about teaching and learning, and reflect a commitment to understanding the relationships among theory, designed artifacts, and practice. At the same time research on specific interventions can contribute to theories of learning and teaching. In DBR, practitioners and researchers work together to produce meaningful change in contexts of practice, for instance, involving classrooms after school programmes, teachers and communities. Such collaboration means that goals and constraints are drawn from the local context as well as the researcher's agenda, addressing one concern of many reform efforts. Emerging such partnerships across multiple sellers can uncover relationships between the numerous variables that come into play in classroom contexts and help refine the key components of intervention.

What are the benefits of DBR?

The benefits of DBR include

- **Practical contribution:** Design-Based Research usually is problem-driven. Researchers seek not only to understand, document and interpret but rather to change and improve educational practices and opportunity. Research results that consider the role of social context and have better potential for influencing educational practice, tangible products, and programs that can be adopted elsewhere. (Barab and Squire, 2004)
- **Theoretical contribution in authentic contexts:** Design-Based Research, as conceived by Brown (1992), was introduced with the expectation that researchers would systemically adjust various aspects of the designed context so that each adjustment served as a type of experimentation that allowed the researchers to test and generate theory in authentic contexts. And research results that are validated through the consequences of their use, providing consequential evidence or validity. (Messick, 1992).
- **Better ties between theory and practices and between researchers and practitioners:** Research should address questions of genuine interest to educators and the findings should also be presented in a way that is useful to practitioners (Reeves, 2000). Design-Based studies take place in suit and rely on the active input and participation at all four stages of practitioners. Design-Based studies bring well-designed interventions (materials, artifacts, and software) and are well situated in the educational field. Indeed, very close interaction between practitioners, researchers, experts, and other stakeholders is essential.
- Improve and generate evidence-based claims about learning. Researchers are finding themselves developing

contexts, frameworks, tools, and pedagogical models to better understand emerging pedagogical theories or ontological commitments (diSessa and Cobb, 2004). In these contexts, the research moves beyond simply observing and actually involves systematically engineering these contexts in ways that allow research participants to improve practice and generate evidence-based claims about learning. The commitment to examining learning interventions in naturalistic contexts, many of which are designed and systematically changed by the researcher, necessitates the development of a methodological toolkit for deriving evidence-based claims from these contexts. (Barab and Squire, 2004)

- **Offer a useful methodological toolkit to those researchers committed to understanding variables within naturalistic contexts:** Design-Based Research is not so much an approach as it is a series of approaches, with the intent of producing new theories, artifacts, and practices that account for and potentially impact learning and teaching in naturalistic settings. (Cobb, diSessa, Lehrer, and Schauble, 2003) stated:

Prototypically, design experiments entail both "engineering" particular forms of learning and systematically studying those forms of learning within the context defined by the means of supporting them. This designed context is subject to test and revision, and the successive iterations that result play a role similar to that of systematic variation in experiment.

For example, this approach can be used for discipline specific tentative research design for data collection, analysis and explanation for a specific field of study. Initial design efforts can be focused on developing software and activity structures to support investigations by the scholars of natural selection, followed by cycles of designs, enactment and analysis to successfully redefine the relationship between technological planning for inquiry and social planning to support scientific discourses. Besides improving curriculum design the study will help yielding facts from findings concerning psychological aspects of scholar's understanding of scientific explanation on the basis of reasoning.

Creative Approaches to Research

Creative Approaches to Research (CAR) is a cross-disciplinary approach in research that reflects the convergence that is now occurring in the fields between epistemology and technology. The approach is electronic and flexible enough to incorporate multiple forms of text including academic and creative writing, sound, images and multimedia. The purpose of the approach is to contribute to the academic discourse on alternative forms of research of the representation. It is underpinned by the epistemological premise that there are multiple ways of experiencing, knowing and communicating. The use of multidimensional research within the approach reflects the notion that there is no single, correct way to have an experience or transmit knowledge of that experience. This approach is designed to be a vehicle for shaping new forms of an academic exploration and expression. Innate in the philosophy of the CAR, this is a continuing questioning about what research is, what it might become and how this approach might best reflect and shape that evaluation. (Brearly, 2008).

Creative Approaches to Research emerged from postmodern theories of reflexivity. Multiplicity and complexity and the doubt that any method or theory has a universal claim of authoritative knowledge (Richardson, 2005) CAR is supported by an epistemological premise that there are multiple ways of experience knowing and communicating. (Japson and Paley, 1997) There is no single, correct way to have an experience or transmit knowledge of that experience. (Lather and Smithies, 1997) Creative Approaches acknowledged our own humaneness as research and research participants and invite levels of engagement that we hope will connect with the humanity in others.

What do Creative Approaches to Research mean for Researchers?

Challenging the shape and appearance of research opens the doors to issues of authority, legitimacy, responsibility and power, which go to the core of how one views the world and what it values. This raises many complexities for researches. There are three of the tensions that creative researches need to learn to work with.

- Knowing the rules and Challenging the assumptions
- Being creative and maintaining rigour
- Honoring content and exploring form

These sets of paired ideas are not dualities. They can be true simultaneously. Many questions emerge from the interplay of these ideas.

Knowing the rules and challenging the assumptions:

- How can we work with a recognised framework of scholarship and challenge its assumption about form?
- How can we stretch the edges of a recognised form and retain its strengths?
- How can we move beyond compliance to an authentic research?

Being creative and maintaining rigour:

- How can we invite emotional engagement with data and avoid sentimentality and self-indulgences?
- How can we invite engagement and avoid pomposity and emotional absence?
- How can we integrate the cerebral and creative

Honouring content and exploring form:

- How can we avoid the form taking over and eclipsing the content?
- How can we creatively enliven content while honouring the original voices?

The sense of excitement that is generated by working in this paradoxical terrain is closely liked to the discomfort that emerges from disintegrating familiar conventions, working in the luminal spaces of creative approaches requires political awareness, good support systems and above all courage. (Brearley, 2008)

The Holy Bible says "In the beginning was the Word, and the Word was with God, and the Word was God". (St. John 1:1) It implies that everything had the beginning from the WORD. Human beings are thinking animals. Thought is nested in speech, not in tests, all of which have their meanings through reference of the visible symbol to the world of sound. Thought and expression in oral cultures is often highly organised but calls for organisation of a sort of unfamiliar to and often uncongenial to the literate mind. This organisation is basically formulaic, structured in proverbs and other set expressions. It is aggregative rather them analytic, participatory rather than distanced, situational rather than abstract. (Org. 1982). The command over arithmetics, astrology, proverbs, etc. which our forefathers were experts through their oral mastery is found lacking in this modern literate world. Most of the known civilisations were having oral culture. Even Iliad and Odyssey were basically oral creations.

Our nation provides ample opportunity for the researchers to apply creative approaches to research and to explore the hidden treasures that are retained by the different tribal groups. Many of the oral or residually oral cultures strike literates as extraordinarily agonistic in their verbal performance and indeed in their life style. That means fit for the context. India is a "Babel of Languages". The variety of languages has been built up through the ages by various races and ethnic groups that made their way into India. There are 18 officially recognised major languages, 1652 languages are spoken as mother tongue (Census of India 1991). While conducting any research among the Tribals one has to apply a Creative Approach to Research by integrating culture, language, history, geography, anthropology, socio-economic conditions that bind them as a community.

Work Integrated Research Learning Approach

Work Integrated Learning (WIL) is gaining a greater profile within higher education today. The purposes of WIL are many and varied. The diverse parties to WIL activity, therefore, students, employers, educators, and professionals bring their own perspectives. There are some basic considerations to be addressed, namely. (1) Whether or not students may be charged fees for courses that have a work-based component to them, (2) Whether the student is simply on work experience in industry, they can only be asked to pay towards the administrative costs borne by the institution in organising and monitoring such experiences, and (3) The institution can claim to be directing and managing the students learning whilst they are engaged in industry activity, their income can flow to the institution in the same way as a conventional institution – based course. e.g. Institution-industry linked programmes; placement, projects with bilateral agreements/collaboration.

Work Integrated Learning Curriculum

Essentially, courses generating student fee revenue should be able to demonstrate that enrolled students are engaged in learning that has all the hallmarks of curriculum design expected of any higher education course, including an articulation of curriculum standards. Work-based courses which do not attract revenue can exercise their discretion over the extent to which student work experience is set within academic curriculum design.

What students emerge with can be understood as the sum total of a multitude of courses they have completed en route. This can be aggregated with various formulae to provide a grade point average or an overall class of degree. With the whole being seen as more than the sum of the parts, a set of courses produces graduate capabilities that the programme is designed to deliver.

Identification of Capabilities

Capabilities are intended to be more integrated and holistic than intellectual prowess in a given field of study (O'Reilly, Cunningham and Lester, 1999). They are about the way we act and the way we have the abilities to do and to be. Capabilities broaden out from the intellectual to include moral education and practice education. Capabilities have an uncertain relation to both 'competencies' and to 'attributes'. Competencies are generally held to be rather more behaviorally and skill oriented. Competencies are measured by their performances. Attributes are largely used to talk about what can be expected of any student, no matter what his field of study.

What students come out with can be thought about in terms of capabilities, or competencies, or attributes – or all three. Some might well argue that a new vocationalism is threatening scholarly traditions (Symes and Mclntyre, 2000), or, that employers and professionals, accrediting bodies are gamming too much sway over the academic programme, and too much grounded in defining what students outcome are desirable (Gonczi, 1994).

Assessment and Student Workplace Learning

One can assess from the comfort of making room the student's display of analytic, critical and reflective capability. The application of pre-determined assessment criteria may help ensure consistency, and grades can be moderated as others view the textual evidence. So, reconciling academic standards with Work Integrated Learning may seem fairly straightforward. These kinds of written assignments bring academic standards under the preview of the institution. If the learning objective is for students to stand aside from the workplace experience and show that they can analyze, critique and reflect from the institution vantage point what they found in the world of work, then perhaps this is a valid way to do it.

The achievement of complex (or divergent or emergent) learning outcomes has become a topic of interest in higher education that seeks to foster "deep learning". The assessment of complex learning is, to coin a phrase, complex (Knight and Banks, 2003). The assessment of complex learning outcomes is placing the spotlight on the exercise of judgment by assessors, the place of tacit knowledge in the expertise that goes into judgment by experienced assessors, and the value of engaging students in learning how to develop judgment making (expertise in assessment) through the assessment process itself (Boud, 2007). Knight and Yorke, (2006) question the extent to which the complex learning associated with workplace environment can be captured in a trustworthy way in summative assessment beyond a pass/fail judgment, which may be required especially where professional accreditation looks for warrants of fitness to practice, limits to trustworthiness have to do with; contingencies impacting on the learning environment; unpredictably of learning outcomes, and variability in the quality of learning resources and processes (involving, among other things, the contribution of workplace supervisors).

Observations from Research Study

From the inquiry, it was found that all planning programmes unequivocally endorsed the importance of practice education. All those who have involved were of the view that professional and practical aspects were fundamental to their programmes, and that practice education/work integrated education has huge benefits for students and employers. There, is a commonly expressed ethos of experiential and reflective learning as underpinning practice education. It involves four main approaches. (1) The provision of brief encounter with practice, (2) Project-based work, (3) Structured work placement, and (4) Work experience.

There is general preference amongst the planning educators that assessment should encourage reflective rather than mechanistic practice. Assessment should foster a critical exploration by students of what they learned through exposure to work and professional contexts, and what in their practice they might improve or do differently. This is seen to be moving beyond understanding and applying workplace skills and competencies. Some placed special weight on the importance of developing ethical practice. The assessment instruments included group work, project reports, seminar presentations, case studies, journals, diaries, reflective reports, planning capabilities portfolios, and employer reports. The less institution-based course, the less likely it was that assessment would be graded pass or fail, (Jones, Jackson and Coote, 2011).

The main aim is to see the students grow in confidence. They are sensitive to the difference in students, from those who seemed naturally comfortable in the workplace to those who are uneasy and diffident. They are concern about the importance of communication, of working alongside others, of learning how to deal with people, and learning how to make decisions. Making decisions and negotiating change are salient themes in planning profession. They require capabilities that are analytic, interpretive, ethical, communicative, and sometimes transformative. Not surprisingly, workplace supervisors largely expressed the view that universities intuitions are about learning to think and workplaces learning to do. (Jones, Jackson and Coote. 2011).

Some planners are prepared to invest highly in students for later benefits. They do not find much time to read and absorb much of the university institution course documentation with which they have been provided. Supervision and feedback largely occurred on the basis of day to day assistance with specific work tasks, 'check in' and getting alongside, perhaps with periodic appointments, and all supported in most instance by team colleagues. Plan would be valuable, preferably with some guidance as to broad areas from which the students would create their individual learning goals. It is taken for granted that the students are benefited in shaping their learning experience within the workplace context, overall, the student assessment is the responsibility of the university institution. (Jones, Jackson and Coote, 2011)

Most students are very positive about the value of their work placement. They feel that it gives them experience of what planners actually do and how they do it. It acts both to introduce them to planning practice and networks for future employment. Work placement may not be a happy experience for everybody. It is found that the knowledge and theory from university institution are part of what they do in the workplace. Students have realised the importance of critical thinking and analysis, and wanted the university institution to forge greater connection between their increased professional competence and their abilities to be critical and reflective practitioners. Their accounts strongly advocated for purposefully linking workplace learning with what comes before and after. (Jones, Jackson and Coote, 2011)

Students are not very clear about the specific goals or benchmarks for them to achieve. Their expectations are often considered to be more general about the quality of work and how to face it. Tasks which enabled them to 'round off' their placement experience, by pulling together their aspirations about the experience or analysing an issue they have encountered, seemed to be particularly appreciated (Jones, Jackson and Coote, 2011).

To conclude, structured work placements bring considerable benefits to students, work places and academic programmes. The work places contexts and the capacities and dispositions of the work place supervisors lend themselves to informal, nurturing assessment practices that encourage students to grow in confidence and professional identity. Work experience by itself does not guarantee learning, at either the surface or deeper levels, it is a matter of how the student engages with that experience and transforms it into a learning journey. Work place supervisors and university institution educators have important roles to play, and students need to be held accountable for the ways in which they go about it. They need to perform, even if the performance is not focused on the demonstration of prescribed competencies but on their engagement with the learning process. The judicious use of accessories such as learning plans, assessment guides, and capability portfolios may support that process and provide important reference points for all parties. The provision of appropriate learning infrastructures for direct intrinsic, formative assessment needs to be based on clear educational principles. (Jones, Jackson and Coote, 2011)

Union Minister for Human Resources Development, Kapil Sibal has spoken in the parliament on Friday, 5th August 2011, to introduce Work Integrated Learning for plus 1 and plus 2 students as well as the students pursuing their undergraduate studies.

Australia's Minister for Tertiary Education, Skills, Jobs and Workplace Relations, Christopher Evans, who visited India during July 2011 is keen on leveraging its vast experience and expertise in vocation training to fill the huge gap in the availability of skilled personnel in India. It should aim to acquire international recognition for work. It is a skill transfer involving industry – real skill valued by employers looking to meet international students.

11

Issues and Challenges in Integrated Education

Education Ideals of the Past

Like Plato in the West, Confucius is lauded for his continuing impact on vast sections of Asia even today. His has an ongoing reputation, almost revered in some sections. In his lifetime, Confucius taught thousands of students and spelled out powerful educational insights that still influence social life in Asia. His ultimate objective, as was Plato's, was transformation not just for the benefit of the individual, but also for all of society. He believed the true quest for knowledge would transform everyone and, thereby, bring about the transformation of all society and the whole world. Like in Plato's case, it is clear that "education for Confucius served a very pragmatic purpose – the creation of individuals who would be able to ensure better government". (Timothy, 2000)

Philosophy

Confucius philosophy is a complex system of moral, social, political, philosophical, and quasi-religious thought that influenced the culture and history of East Asia. Confucius stated it succinctly, "tell me, and I will forget; show me, and I may remember; involve me, and I will understand". His goal was to reform the government, and his goals for education were to produce those who were capable to serve in government in decisive roles. He attempted to produce 'chuntgu', which is quite similar to the English word "gentleman". The system aimed at producing people of character using observation, study and reflective thought in the process.

Confucius said that "liking to know is better than just having to know, enjoying knowing is much better than just liking to know. That means people often do not want to do it, even they know it is right. If people like it, they may do it, but they cannot keep going. If people love it, they must do it. Because the whole of mind, body and feeling want to do it. They are strong enough to do it". It is hard for them to give up. The saying of Confucius can help us to understand why students do not do it sometimes even though they have known what their teachers or parents said is absolutely right. In other words, if there are no arts and beauty in the world, ethics will become a kind of very boring knowledge. According to this, we can understand why we have a long history of moral education in ancient China, and India but we have failed in it finally. A lot of people do not really follow the moral way. For them, the thing that their reason may want to do is not what their feelings want to do. So they do not get strong enough to do it. They have to fail to it, even when saying they want to do it. (Fan, 2004)

Dewey, like Plato and Confucius, placed education strongly within the community setting and believed that learning was an intensely social process involving people and their customs, institutions, beliefs, victories and defeats, recreations and occupations. This was a continuous process: 'The continuity of any experience, through renewing of the social group, is a literal fact'. Further, 'Education, in its broadest sense, is the means of this social continuity of life'. (Dewey, 1916)

A casual glimpse into those systems could offer some valuable lessons that can be applied to or incorporated into our education today. Early eastern educational methods tended to emerge from everyday life. There were real connections between what was learnt and the lives that were lived. Although these systems were based primarily on religion, they were less fragmented and, hence, more integrated and related to real life. This was probably because religion and life itself were so closely intertwined as a whole.

In India, education began with the teaching of traditional elements such as Indian religions, culture, arts, mathematics, medicine, logic, and other subjects useful in real life. Early Hindu and Buddhist centres of learning, such as Takshila and Nalanda, were well-known for their higher levels of education drawing people from all over the world. Although educational models in Ancient Asia were heterogeneous, reflecting the influence and teachings of major philosophical, cultural, and religious traditions of Hinduism, Buddhism, Islam, and Confucianism, there was a much clearer real-life connection than we see today. Formal learning was employed, but it had direct and clear objectives. Traditions had to be preserved, professions had to be passed on to younger generations, harmony in community had to be restored, religious practices had to be observed, and children needed to be taught the right things for growing up in their community. For example, Confucius aimed to reform society and governance, and for that, the goal of education had to be to nurture capable persons who could serve in decisive roles in the government.

Education Today

While rapid changes are taking place in education today within the institution, learning in real life is not yet met with. Within our global context, with the rapid pace at which knowledge is increasing, the problem has less to do with the content of our educational models, and more with the methods and the need for an appropriate learning environment. The need is for building up a conducive setting for real learning to take place-one that would produce positive results in the learners within our changing world. Such a setting must be rooted in reality, which most modern educational systems are found wanting. (Dharampal, 1983)

A recent trend contributing to the exploitation of the learning environment is the heavy focus on 'job-orientation'. Here one is speaking purely from the point of view of the real value of education, although this could be a positive trend with focused skill-oriented training. But, if all learning is tailored to the requirements of a particular profession-focused on acquiring the required skills and specific knowledge base, then the student misses out on the larger picture of life itself. Students do not come out as well-rounded individuals. (Gnanakan, 2011)

Integrated Education

Integrated education is defined as education that promotes learning and teaching in non-fragmented ways that embrace notions of holism, complexity, and interconnection. Integrated education rejects the common emphasis on transmitted knowledge. Rather, it proposes that knowledge and meaning are constructed by the learner through processes of interaction with others, the material, and the social and physical contexts. Integrated education calls to question the traditional gulfs between teacher and learner, and rejects the divisions between physiology, cognition, and emotion in the learning process. Furthermore, it embraces the links, rather than the divisions, between the academic disciplines (such as, arts and sciences) and between various subjective and objective epistemologies and methods of inquiry. Other terms used are integrative learning, integrated curriculum, interdisciplinary teaching, transformational learning, thematic teaching, and synergistic teaching.

Speaking of integration is in keeping with current trends where words such as 'holism' and 'synergy' are in vogue. Holism, to start with, is a much misunderstood word in various fields of study today. We have Holistic Medicine or Holistic Management and could dismiss it as something on the fringes of society. But the term 'holism' is being employed frequently even in contemporary academic conversations, and is one with an underlying reference to integration. The term is derived from the Greek word *holos* meaning 'whole'. But, importantly, holism refers to something even more than the whole. The Oxford English Dictionary defines holism as the 'tendency in nature to form wholes that are more than the sum of the parts by ordered grouping'. Basically, holism refers to the theory that the parts of any whole cannot exist, nor be understood, except within their relation to the whole. This theory emphasises both the whole and the interdependence of its parts, and underlines the fact that the combined effect of the interaction of two or more forces is greater than the sum of their individual effects. In education, integration is therefore related to why and how the various components of education namely, subjects, teacher, classroom, student, syllabus, and real life are held together. It is in this interconnectedness that must be the foundation for an integrated approach to learning and life. "The highest function of education is to bring about an integrated individual who is capable of dealing with life as a whole". (Gnanakan, 2011)

It was Maria Montessori, the Italian educator, who demonstrated that children are capable of learning the things that they need to know as long as they have the right environment. Her bold claim was that children learn more, directly, from their own environment and less from listening to a teacher talking to the class. The second aspect of integrated learning is the integration of academic knowledge or theoretical concepts in real life. This does not take any specialised effort or skill. The third aspect of integration is to ensure that learning is related to the particular gift of the learner. Not all of us grasp concepts equally well, nor do all of us enjoy accumulating facts and figures. It is important to identify the learners likes and dislikes as these are part of the individual make-up that makes learning personal. Gardner's theory (1993) of multiple intelligences suggests that each individual possesses varying levels of different intelligences. A fourth aspect of integration is the interrelation of one area of learning with another, to break down the walls we have built in our artificially segregated curricula. We have put subjects in unrelated compartments. A learner would learn better if it connects what is learnt in one particular situation or discipline to another. The fifth aspect of integration is that it must employ various modes of delivering education, even those transcending the classroom, for total learning to take place. A variety of other environments for integrated learning need to be explored. All kinds of formal and informal, campus and off-campus, online and offline methods must be utilised to maximise the process of integrated education.

Needless to say, the value of education should also be seen in its role in imparting values. For too long we have looked at education only in terms of acquiring knowledge and skills, and so even teachers are only seen as those who can transfer these components of education. If values or morals were to be transmitted, those were treated as separate subjects. This is where the concept of integration in education would make a difference that proves beneficial. Rather than having an extra subject called 'Moral Science', morals and values should find their place in history, in language, mathematics, in science, and other fields of study.

The urgent need to look at holistic, interconnected, and non-fragmented models that are integrated into real life are to be recognised. One of the drawbacks we face in India is the huge disconnect between central and state government-controlled education, and government-and private-run institutions, as well as gaps that exist within states and cities. Some private agencies are making efforts to bring in changes and bridge these gaps, but by and large the task is titanic.

So, integrated education promotes learning and teaching in non-fragmented ways. It is built on concepts such as synergy, holism, and inter-connectedness. Integrated education embraces learning modes within real life, making real connections within known social and physical contexts. The whole learning experience is seen as one whole, because a human being is a whole person. Teachers are encouraged to create learning environments where children can feel at home rather than in a strange atmosphere school that is alien to their psyche.

Integrated Curriculum

Holism and synergy are essential to integrated education. To consider Dewey's emphasis on experiential learning, or Whitehead's stress on process and interconnectedness, there is a chain of thought that runs through all these educationists and it is integration. Education must be connected to real life; the subjects must be seen as belonging to each other; and above all, the parts must be considered only in their relationship to the bigger whole and its other parts. Moreover, all these must be set in the real world. This leads us to the matter of the curriculum. A host of very lively themes can be drawn from current affairs, culture, tradition and the context. The second way is interdisciplinary integration in which teachers organise the curriculum around common learning across disciplines. They chunk together the common learning embedded in the disciplines to emphasise interdisciplinary skills and concepts. The third way is the transdisciplinary approach in which teachers organise the curriculum around learner's questions and concerns. Learners develop life skills as they apply interdisciplinary and disciplinary skills in real-life contexts.

They share their learning with one another in a community-based learning experience. The learning value is maximum as students, with the minimum effort, make connections among different subject areas and answer various questions as they apply their learning to real-life situation. This kind of integration is far ahead of the regular class-room approach where learners have been seen as knowledge accumulators or depositories, as Freire describes it.

The teacher's role is no longer to control learning but to facilitate it. However, the teacher becomes a facilitator. Teachers need to be gradually introduced to this new paradigm and enabled to accept it. Freire finds that the dialogue of the elite is vertical, whereas true dialogue is a horizontal relationship based on love, respect, and tolerance, which encourages liberated learning in all situations. True education is a lot more than handing down a pre-packaged programme that is often alien to the learner. It is a two-way or multi-directional interactive dialogue, rather than a unilateral authoritarian process that only serves to stifle individuality rather than releasing the individual's potential. (Gnanakan, 2011)

Education as a Process

Whitehead's dynamic approach to education as a process adds an important perspective to our integrated and holistic perspective. Romance provides the initial interest and energy for the learner to enjoy any particular subject. This kind of affectionate love-relationship with the subject-matter is needed to motivate the child to enter the lifelong process of education. Next in the process is the stage of precision, which concerns itself with more thoroughly developing the child's particular interest, rather than merely continuing in the initial romantic phase. The final stage is mastery that brings about the learner's awareness about something has been accomplished. The continuity of the learning process ensures that their interest is built upon to a point where even dry or difficult parts of a text are mastered. Therefore, education is an orchestrated, continuous growing process, in which both learners and subject-matter move progressively to higher levels. They learn best when the new material fits in with what they already know from their real-life context. The education process, has been concerned about fitting together various disjointed pieces that otherwise never seemed to be together. When experience is a orchestrated whole, the learning process becomes more and more an integrated part of each learner.

Community Learning

Education institutions can become small self-sufficient communities that are part of the larger rural community. Learning was, therefore, placed within the context of real life, that is, within the community. What is lacking in most learning environments is the human relationship element of a living community. If one makes learning a part of community and give it a relational element, then human relations would need to be considered as being essential for the learning process. Communities are extensions of individuals and individuals are extensions of their inner identities, and all these need to be integrated to make a dynamic learning process.

The child operates optimally in non-threatening circumstances and when learning becomes part of real-life community interactions, community bonds, mutual trust, and shared discourse are attributes that enable the human brain to function best, as any physiologist would confirm. Thus, when we create a conducive learning environments within positive, supportive human relationships, and where individuals feel a sense of belonging, the learning value is enhanced multifold. (Dewey, 1915)

Morals and values should find an integral place in all of life. Consequently, as part of educational programmes, morals and values have to be integrated with every form of intelligence and in every human action. Integration is all about living and, therefore, when learning is integrated with life, we become alive to all the challenges of our multifaceted world.

Issues and Challenges in Integrated Education

One of the developments in Integrated Education is to strike a proper balance between didactic training (knowing from reading and studying) and 'skills' (broadly the ability to do things well); a major departure from essentially 'learning' centric offering at present. The 'skill' portfolio needs to be flexible and expansive with provision for acquiring 'multiple' and more importantly 'switchable' skills along with essential disciplinary expertise. Since there are limits to the range of 'skills' that can be imparted within the time domain and framework of a structured program, the best course is to equip every learner with a set of 'core skills' that can be returned and amplified to enable adaptation to emerging opportunities and challenges in the rapidly changing world.

A possible wish list would include 'skills' innumeracy (quantitative/analytical thinking), language, communication and networking, accessing and managing information (data mining) and imbibing the spirit of competitiveness and innovation (out-of-the box view of things). These attributes of 'core skills' essential for employment, entrepreneurship, knowledge and wealth creation are not to be viewed as contradictory but are inherently complementary in the pursuit of learning for scholarship, disciplinary expertise and intellectual enrichment. Acquisition of 'core skills' and adequate exposure to basic courses are necessary for Integrated Education. (Padmashree, 2008)

Dynamic Synergy between Learning and Skills

A Paradigm shift in undergraduate education and the need to design a new learning system for the first degree, to produce millions of graduates every year is the main stay of our Higher Education system. A national aspiration that every graduate should not only have disciplinary knowledge but also armed with a set of essential skills is absolutely necessary for education in the 21st century. To be able to deliver on such an ambition, there will have to be a tectonic shift from the traditional teaching programme to equip every learner vis-a-vis the needs and expectations of the knowledge and skills driven competitive regime that dominates the real world.

Quality Enhancement

Our education system suffers from the entrenched tendency to import rote learning may have some shock value to those who believe that private educational institutions place greater emphasis on quality and holistic or integrated education. However, for those who closely observe the education scenario, it is a reaffirmation of a bitter truth. Our institutions, by and large, quite far from seeing education as a process of learning with understanding, acquiring knowledge through self discovery and conceptualisation, rather, education remains a mere transmission of information in a rigid classroom atmosphere, where the emphasis is on memorisation and the objective is to rush through a pre-determined syllabus and prepare the students for examination.

A disturbing deficit of social sensitivity on the part of a sizable section of students is another factor to consider, responses to some questions relating to the education of girls and attitudes towards immigrants, the disabled, and HIV positive patients, indicated biases that could, overtime, grow into prejudices.

Despite increasing awareness that learning is not mere information accumulation and that teaching ought to be recast into a facilitation of children's discovery of their own potential and understanding the emphasis on practice continue to be on text books and exams, conceptual understanding is not encouraged sufficiently enough, and sports, arts, debates and cultural activities are kept at a distant periphery. It is time not merely for fostering greater awareness about the need for holistic and integrated education but also to chalk out more imaginative pedagogic means to make education an inclusive an quality centric epistemic process.

Higher education today is undergoing a radical change, posing new-age challenges to universities and institutions. The role of teachers and educators has gone through a metamorphosis as technology and globalisation redefine the contours of the world. With access to information – anywhere, anytime – knowledge today is no longer restricted to physical classrooms. In fact, the real learning is happening laterally, outside the four walls of schools, colleges and universities. "Most of the learning now takes place outside the classroom; through the internet and social media sites". Considering the way technology has changed the education landscape, experts working in the area of education believe that first and foremost, the traditional mindset has to change. That can help the academic community to perceive the future needs of a student going through this transition.

In the digital age, when most of the learning takes place through video games, blogs and social media, we need to see things differently. Plagiarism is a serious concern today. Schools and universities are installing software to find out the correct source. "We need to understand that the world is not about retaining facts are free, but the world is about deciding which facts are true and correct", The future roadmap of higher education, the academic world agrees, needs to include blended methodology, lifelong learning, collaborative efforts in research and curriculum development, introduction of transnational accreditation agencies and increased student mobility. (Malinis and Tirna, 2011)

Some Observations

Changes are happening in Education worldwide. Sometimes it has been changed, and sometimes changed back. But the end result may not be found significant. There are big variations in educational standards between countries. These have been measured by programmes for International Student Assessment (PISA). PISA findings reveal the need to do three things: get the best teachers, get the best out of teachers; and step in when pupils start to lag behind, it means, the quality of teachers affects student performance more than anything else.

Mckinsey, a consultancy argues that the best performing education systems nevertheless manage to attract the best. In Finland all new teachers must have a master's degree. South Korea recruits primary school teachers from the top 5% of graduates, Singapore and Hong Kong from the top 30%. For curriculum development, in Japan and Finland, groups of teachers visit each others classrooms and plan lessons together. In Finland, they get an afternoon off a week for this. In Boston USA, schedules are arranged so that those who teach the same subject have free classes together for common planning. Examination system and testing varies very much from country to country. While talking about value systems, Singapore has high status because of Confucian values, or that Asian pupils are well behaved and attentive for cultural reasons.

Implications for Integrated Education

The emergence of a large number of interdisciplinary integrated programme of studies such as biotechnology, information technology, management studies, material sciences and econometrics has also brought in considerable change in the academic programme of institutions. These interdisciplinary areas and their related technologies are transforming life, and the culture of society as a whole. Besides the novelty, other utility in the industrial and service sectors and the consequent growth in demand for well-trained employees in those areas in the new socio-economic order have made higher education institutions to formulate academic programme by applying an integrated approach.

In brief institutions of higher learning are today pressurised to move away from the traditional understanding of the term 'knowledge' which emphasised on language, especially through writing, an open process of communication and formal and discipline- bound conventions. Institutions should move on to the new understanding of knowledge through action, particular outcomes of learning and trans-disciplinary skills. Only through such initiatives, can institutions assist society with the incorporation of the country into the global economy. The challenge, therefore, is how effectively and how quickly will there be a move away from traditional university- type institutions that establish a range of basic social values, and discipline-based and knowledge-based basic academic skills to a new type of universities and institutions that produce flexible all-rounders. Today both institution and student should also move away from their preoccupation with examinations. When the emphasis has shifted from knowledge to skills and competencies, present day examinations will have lost their relevance, as they will not indicate the overall achievement of students in terms of skills both cognitive and general as well as subject related knowledge. (Dutta, 2007)

These changes are common to all societies of the world and the cumulative effect of all these changes demand a different type of human resources, ones that are different from what the higher education institutions have been preparing in the past. Consequently, higher education institutions are under pressure to play different roles that are different from traditional ones. Significant among these new responsibilities are:

- Providing educational programme of new models based on flexibility and learner choice.
- Preparing students for the information era by developing the skills for information processing.
- Preparing students for lifelong learning by developing an appropriate learning style among them.
- Providing for adult and non-formal education to increase percentage of mature learners
- Providing for specialised skill-oriented courses of different levels.
- Catering to the demand of the international market
- Maintaining quality in all the above endeavours
- Optimising the available resources to facilitate quality output.

That means knowledge and training of high quality that would be of use in any society in the world irrespective of regional and socio economic variances. In addition, the extent and quality of these components should be at an internationally acceptable level. These two basic elements of world class education, namely, relevance and excellent quality, need to be ensured. The seamlessness between disciplines and professions is yet another manifestation of internal and external globalisation of integrated higher education. Therefore, potential students should become interdisciplinary, multidimensional to fit into the changing world. It will challenge one to think out of the box in which the old fashioned education has prepared us. A shift from conventional, information based education to knowledge based education is essential for one to be part of global economy. (Chopra, 2008).

Education institutions need to do three things; get the best teachers; get the best out of teachers; and step in when pupils to start to lag behind. The quality of teachers affects students performance more than anything else. The best performing education systems nevertheless manage to attract the best. Having got good teaches, there is a temptation to show them into classrooms and let them get on with it. For understandable reasons, teachers rarely get much training in their own classrooms. But, successful experiments can still do much to overcome the difficulty.

Bibliography

Abdul Kalam, A.P.J., (2007), Banaras Hindu University, Convocation Address, Varanasi.

Abdul Kalam, A.P.J., (2007), Capacity Building among Universities, University News, 5(21), New Delhi.

Abdul Kalam, A.P.J., (2007), Technology is a Non Linear Tool, University News, 45(18), New Delhi.

Aggarwal, J.C., (2005), Basic Ideas in Education, Shipra Publication, New Delhi.

Aggarwal, J.C., (2004), Philosophical and Sociological Perceptives on Education, Shipra Pub., New Delhi.

Ahluwalia J.S., (2001), Higher Education in the 21st Century, Keynote Address, Punjabi University, Patiala.

Aide Santiago Acosta, (2010), *Values and Virtues in the Era of Globalisation*, University News, 48(39), New Delhi.

Alfred North Whitehead, (1967), Science and the Modern World, The Free Press, New York.

Amanda Mergler, (2008), 'Making the Implicit Explicit: Values and Morals in Queensland Teachers Education'. *Australian Journal of Teacher Education,* 33(4), August.

Arati Sen., (2004), Education in Human Values: Vision of Rabindranath Tagore, Value Development in Higher Education, New Delhi.

Babu S., (2007), Technological Advances and Role of ICT in Teacher Training and Higher Education, University News, 45(26), New Delhi.

Barab, S. and Squire, B., (2004). “Design-Based Research: Putting a Stake in the Ground.” *The Journal of the Learning Sciences, 13* (1), 1-14. Retrieved March, 2006 fromhttp://website.education.wisc.edu/kdsquire/manuscripts/jls-barab-squire-design.pdf

Battacharya, I. and Sharma, K. (2007), ‘India in the Knowledge Economy an Electronic Pardigm’, International Journal of Educational Management, Vol. 21, No. 6.

Bhattacharya, Ashoke (2008): Grundtvig, Tagore, Gandhi and Paulo Freire, Their Educational Thought: viewed from Third World Perspective., Readers Service, New Delhi.

Bikas C. Sanyal, D.N., (2008), Globalisation and Higher Education: Implications for India, University News, 46(36), New Delhi.

Biswas.N.B. and Deka Mouchuni, (2011), Tagore and Gandhi on Education: A Research perspective, University News, 49(20), New Delhi.

Bloom, Allan, (1987), The Closing of American Mind, Simon and Schuster, New York.

Blurton, C., (2002), New Directions of ICT – Use in Education, Available http://www.unesco.org/education/educprog/lwf/dl/edict.pdf.

Bonds, C., Cox, C. and Gantt-Bonds, L. (1993), “Curriculum Wholeness through Synergistic Teaching.” The Clearing House.

Boud, D. (2007), Reframing Assessment as if Learning were Important. In Boud. D. and Falcmikov. N. (eds.) Rethinking Assessment in Higher Education: Learning for the Long term, Rutledge, London.

Brandreth Gyles., (1984), *The Complete Public Speaker*, Sudha Publications Pvt., Ltd., New Delhi.

Branford, J. (ed.), (1999), How People Learn: Brain, Mind, Experience and School, National Research Council, Washington DC.

Brown, A.L. (1992), Design Experiments: Theoretical and Methodological Challenges in Creating Complex Interventions in Classroom Settings. *Journal of the Learning Sciences, 2*(2).

Bush, M.B., (1974), First Survey of Education. Published by Centre of Advanced study in Education, Faculty of Education and Psychology, M.S. University of Baroda, Baroda.

Bush, M.B., (1974): First Survey Report of Education. Society for Educational Research and Development, Ahmedabad.

Bush, M.B., (198-88), Fourth Survey of Research in Education Vol. I, Publication Department by the Secretary NCERT, Sri Aurobindo Marg, New Delhi.

Byrne, H.W. ed. (1981), D.A. Christian Approach to Education, Zondervan, Grand Rapids.

Carver, Rebecca, (2001), Continuity and Interaction in the Context of Practice, Seattle W.A.

Cenkner, William, (1989), The Hindu Personality in Education, New Delhi.

Chakrabarti Mohit, (1997), Value Education: Changing Perspectives, Kauishka Publications, New Delhi.

Chopra, K.L., (2008), Some Life Style Commandments for Knowledge Era Populace, University News, 46(48), New Delhi.

Christopher Ball, (2009), Perspectives on the Future Learning by Emily Taylor and Tony Scheehan; http://www ashridge.org.uk

Cisler, S., (2002), Planning for Sustainability: "How to keep your ICT Project Running". http://wwwl.etcnet.org/etc/CisLer/Sustain.doc.

Colling, Patricia, (1974), Dissertation Abstracts International, The Humanities and Social Sciences, University Microforms, Helen Greenway, Vol. 35, No. 5. Michigan.

Colling, Patricia, (1976), Dissertation Abstracts International, The Humanities and Social Sciences, University Microforms, Helen Greenway, Vol. 35, No. 5. Michigan.

Collins, Alan, Diana Joseph and Katerine Bielaczyc, (2004), Design Research: Theoretical and Methodological Issues, *The Journal of the Learning Sciences*, 13(1), 15-42.

Consortium for School Networking, "Taking TCO to the Classroom". Available from http://ctap.fcoe.k12m,ca.us/ctap/dhs3.4/tco2class.pdf

Cousins, N.E., (1991), *Process Theology*, Newman Press, New York.

Covaleskie, John, F., Dewey, Discipline and Democracy; http://www.ed.uinc.edu//EPs/PEs-year book/94-docs/COVALESK* HTM.

David Ackerman and D.N. Perkins (1989), "Integrating Thinking and Learning Skills Across the curriculum" In Heldi Hayes Jacobs, ed., Interdisciplinary Curriculum: Design and Implementation, Association for Supervision and Curriculum Development.

David, S.A., Sanyal, B.C. and Wildemeersch, D., (2007), Engaging with Cross-border Higher Education in India While Sustaining the Best Tradition of Indian Values, University News, 45(37), New Delhi.

Dewey, John, (1938), Experience and Education, Macmillan Publishing Company, New York.

Dewey, John (1915), The School and Society, University of Chicago Press, Chicago Gardner, Howard E. (1993), Frames of Mind: The Theory of Multiple Intelligences, Basic Books, New York.

Dewey, John, (1938), *Experience and Education (EE),* MacMillan Publishing Company, New York.

Dewey, John, (1944), Democracy and Education (DE), The Free Press, New York.

Dewey, John, (1957), Reconstruction in Philosophy, (RP), Beacon Press, Boston

Dewey, John, (1964), The School and Society and The Child and the Curriculum (SSCC), The University of Chicago Press, Chicago.

Dewey, John, (1989), Freedom and Culture (FC), Prometheus Books, Buffalo.

Dewey, John, (1991), How We Think (HWT), Prometheus Books, Buffalo.

Dewey, John, (1997), Democracy and Education: An Introduction to the Philosophy of Education, The Free Press, New York. Available at http://en.wikisource.org/wiki/ Democracy- and-Education, accessed on 5 October 2010, p. 5.

Dhawan, Gopinath, (1990), The Philosophy of Mahatma Gandhi, The Gandhi Peace Foundation, 58, New Delhi.

diSessa, A., and Cobb, P., (2004). "Ontological innovation and the role of theory in design experiments." *Journal of the Learning Sciences,* 13 (1), Retrieved March, 2006 from http:/ /inkido.indiana.edu/design/disessa.doc

Dutta, Krishna and Andrew Robinson, (1995), Rabindranath Tagore: The Myriad-Minded Man, Bloomsbury, London.

Dutta, P.K., (2007), Quality Higher Education in India, University News, Vol. 45(19). New Delhi.

Dutta, P.K., (2007), Quality Maintenance in Higher Education, University News, 45(31), New Delhi.

Dutta, P.K., (2007), Quality Maintenance in Higher Education, University News 45(31), New Delhi.

Fouts, J., (2002), Research on Computers and Education: Past, Present and Future, available from http://www.gates foundation.org/nr/downloads/ed/evaluation/Computer Research Summary.pdf;

Gnanakan, Ken, (2007), Learning in an Integrated Environment, Theological Book Trust, Bangalore.

Gnanakan, Ken, (2011), Integrated Learning, Oxford University Press, New Delhi.

Gonezi. A.,(1994), Competency Based Assessment in Professions in Australia, Assessment in Education, 1 (1), 27-44.

Good, C., (Ed.), (1973), Dictionary of Education, Third Edition. McGraw Hill, New York.

Government of India (2009), National Knowledge Commission: Report to the Nation, NKC, GOI, New Delhi.

Government of India (2009), Report of the Committee on Renovation and Rejuvenation of Higher Education in India, GOI, New Delhi.

Government of India Youth Policy on Education, (1988), New Delhi.

Gregory, S., (2006), University News, 45(24), New Delhi.

Grover, Verinder (1994), Rabindranath Tagore, Deep and Deep Publication New Delhi.

Gupta, B.L., (2010), Audit the Learning Resources, University News, Vol.48(2), New Delhi.

Haddad, Wadi D. and Jurich, Sonia (2002), "ICT for Education: Potential and Potency", in Haddad. W and Dvexler. A (eds). Technologies for Education, Parameters and Prospects, Washington, DC.

Haddad, W. and Drexler, A. (eds.), (2002), Technologies of Education: Potentials, Parameters, and Prospects, Washington, DC.

Harijan, (1987) May 8, Wardha.

Harsch, E.D., (1987), Cultural Literacy, Houghton Mifflin Company, Boston.

Hawkins, R., (2002), "Ten Lessons for ICT and Education in the Developed World", available from http://www.cid.haryard.edu/cr/pdf/gitrr2002

(http://www.enlacequiche.org.gt/english/vision.htm) (2009).

Howard Woodhouse, (1995), Towards a Process Theory of Learning "Feel the Beauty of the World," Interchange, Vol.26/4.

Hume Robert, E., (2002), *The Thirteen Principal Upanishads*, Oxford University Press, New Delhi.

Iamagna Carmen, Z and Villanueva Charles, (2010), *Higher Education Values Across Time and Culture: Survival or Revival?,* University News, 48(39), New Delhi.

IESALC – UNESCO, (2008), Ana Lucia Gazzola and Axel Didriksson (ed.) *Trends in Latin American and Caribbean Higher Education*, Caracas.

ILO Report (2002), Geneva.

In 1992, Whitehead generalised his educational ideas in a Pamphlet, "The Rhythm of Education" Franz G. Riffert expounds these thoughts in "Alfred North Whitehead on Learning and Education: Theory and Application." New York.

Information Technology in Higher Education; AIU, 2000 Annual reports of Various Apex Academic Institutions, New Delhi.

Japson, J. and Paley, N., (eds.) (1997), Daredevice Research; Recreating Analytic Practice, Peter Lang Publishing, New York.

Jha, Narmadeshwar, (1994), UNESCO: International Bureau of Education, Vol. XXIV, 603(19), Paris.

John, Murray, (1961), Rabibdranath Tagore, the Pioneer in Education, London.

Joshi, M.M. (1998), H.E. in India, Vision and Action, Country Paper, UNESCO Conference on HE in 21st Century, Paris.

Joshi, M.M., (2010), MIC, HRD, Government of India Global Student Mobilisation Report, IDP, New Delhi.

Karpaga, Vinayagam M., (2007), The Prime Goal of Education, University News, 45(3), New Delhi.

Kathleen, O'Connell, (2002), Rabindranath Tagore: The Poet as Educator, Visva Bharathi, Calcutta.

Kathy, Lake, (1973), Integrated Curriculum, School Improvement Research Series.

Keegan, Dermond, (2002), The Future of Learning: "From e-learning to M-learning", Information Analysis; Opinion Papers.

Khanolkar, G.D., (1996), The Lute and The Plough: A Life of Rabindranath Tagore, and The Book Centre Private Ltd., Bombay.

Knight, P.T. and Banks, W., (2003), The Assessment of Complex learning outcomes, Global journal of Engineering Education, 7 (1).

Kripalani, Krishna, (1980), Rabindranath Tagore, Visvabharati, Calcutta.

Lam Paul and Mc Naught Carmel, (2007), Management of an e-learning Evaluation Project: The e-learning Model, Journal of Interactive Learning Research, Vol. 18, No. 3.

Lanra, Brearley (2008), Introduction to Creative Approaches to Research, RMIT Publishing, http://www.rmitpublishing.com.au/car.html

Lipson, Valencia, S., Wixson, K., and Peters, C. (1993), "Integration and Thematic Teaching: Integration to Improve Teaching and Learning." Language Art.

Littlejohn, Allison, *et al.* (2009), Characterising Effective e-learning Resources, Computers and Education, Vol. 50(3).

Lo, Ping-Cheng, (1999), *Confucian Ethics of Death with Dignity and the Contemporary Relevance*, Society of Christian Ethics.

Lokanadha Reddy C. and Mythily, K. (2007), Universities and Extension in the Context of Globalisation, University News, 45 (18), New Delhi.

Mac Dougall, A., and Creed, A., (1997), "A Framework for Reviewing Teacher Professional Development Programmes in Information Technology", Cited in Blurton, C. "New Directions of ICT – use in Education.

Mackinsey and Co., Oct. (2007), How to be Top, The Economist, London.

Magotra R., (2007), Higher Education in the Context of Globalisation, University News, 45(21), New Delhi.

Malcolm D. Evans, (1998), Whitehead and Philosophy of Education; The Seamless Court of Learning, Value Inquiry Book, Amsterdam, Atlanta.

Malhotra, S.P., (2009), Epistemological Issues Related to Quality Research in Education, University News, 47 (29), New Delhi.

Mandke, P., (2007), Promoting Culture of Research in Universities, University News, 45(21), New Delhi.

Martyn, Jones, John, Jackson and Matthew, Coote, (2011), Academic Standards for Work Integrated Learning; a Case

Study from Urban and Regional Planning, Royal Melbourne Institute of Technology University, Melbourne.

Maurer, Richard E., Needham Heights, M.A., (1994), Designing interdisciplinary Curriculum in Middle Junior High, and High Schools, Allyn and Bacon.

Meijun, Fan, (2004), The Idea of Integrated Education from the Point of View of Whitehead's Philosophy of Education, The Council for Global Integrative Education, Sauta Cruz, C.A.

Mool Chand Sharma, (2008), Science, Technology and Globalisation: Challenges and Opportunities for Human Development, University News, 46(36), New Delhi.

Moorehead, Caroline, (1992), Bertrand Russel: A Life, Viking. Westbrook, New York.

Mukherjee, Himangshu Bhushan (1962), Education for Fullness, Asia Publishing House, New Delhi.

Muthuchamy and Thiyagu, (2010), Role of ICT in the Governance of Higher Education, University News 48, (48) New Delhi.

Narasimhamurthy, B.N., (2005), *Satyam Shivam Sundaram*, Vol.5, Sri Sathya Sai Books and Publications Trust, Prasanthi Nilayam

Nayana Tara S., (2007), Quality Assurance in Higher Education: Mission (IM) Possible, University News, 45(28), New Delhi.

NIEPA, (2005), Report of the CABE Committee on Financing Higher and Technical Education: NIEPA, June.

Nitin J. Vyas, (2009), To be an Individual is to be Global: A Cultural Quest in Convergence, University News 47(15), New Delhi.

O'Reilly, D., Cunnigham, L., and Lester, S. (eds.) (1999), Developing the Capable Practitioner; Professional Capability through Higher Education, Kogan page, London.

Outlook, (2007), 30, April, Bombay.

Padmashree, G.M., (2008), Be Creators, Entrepreneurs and Innovators, University News, 46(39), New Delhi.

Panda, B.N., and Pradhan N., (2007), Internationalisation of Quality Higher Education in India: Challenges and Future Perspectives University News, 45(34), New Delhi.

Pani, S.P. and Satpathy, Geeta, (2011), Educational Ideals: The West and India, University News, 49(6), New Delhi.

Pani, R.N. (1986), Integral Education, Thought and Practice, Ashish Publishing House, New Delhi.

Pani, S.P., and Satpathy, Geeta, (2011), Educational Ideals: The West and India, University News, 49(6), New Delhi.

Piar Chand, Yogesh Gupta, Meenakshi Sooden and Sanjeev Kumar, (2007), Impact of Globalisation on Higher Education in India, University News, 45(46), New Delhi.

Power, K.B., (2005), GATS and Higher Education: An Indian Perspective, New Delhi.

Prospects, (1994), The Quarterly Review of Education, UNESCO: International Bureau of Education. Vol. XXIV, No. 3/4, Paris.

Purushothman and Antony Stella, (1995), *Education Innovations*, New Delhi.

Rashmi Banga, (2007), Indian Service Sector: 'Inviting growth with Open arms', The Analyst, January.

Rastogi, S., (2007), Meeting Challenges of ODL System in India, University News, 45(15), New Delhi.

Reagan, Timothy G., (2000), Non-Western Educational Traditions: Alternative Approaches to Educational Thought and Practice, Lawrence Erlbaum Associates.

Ritu Malgotra, (2007), Higher Education in the Context of Globalisation, University News, 46(21), New Delhi.

Robert, (1991), John Dewey and American Democracy, Cornell University Press, Ithica.

Robertson, R., (1992), *Globalisation: Social Theory and Global Culture*, Sage, London.

Rubio Luis Miguel Romeroy Maria Jose, (2004), *Quality and Values in Distance Education,* VIII Distance Education Congress: CREED MEDCOSUR/SUL, Cordoba, Argentina.

Sahni, Sanjay, (2007), *Value Orientation of Higher Education: Integrating Values in Commerce Education*, University News, 45 (24), New Delhi.

Sam Daniel P. and Aroma G. Sam, (2005), Globalisation – New Challenges to Education in India, Prof. V.B. Jagale, World Trade Organisation and Indian Economic Reforms, Serial Publications, Delhi.

Sam Daniel P., (2007), Integrated Learning, Symposium on Pedagogical Approach to Comparative Religion and Philosphy, Dravidian University, Kuppam.

Sansanwal, D.N., (2007), Strategies of Universities in the Globalisation Process, University News, 46(38), New Delhi.

Selected Letters of Rabindranath Tagore, (1997), edited by Krishna Dutta and Andrew Robinson.

Sen A, (2004), Education in Values: Vision on Rabindranath Tagore, Value Development in Higher Education, Viva Books Private Ltd, New Delhi.

Sen Malini and Tay Tirna, (2011), Towards Tomorrow, The Times of India, December 5, Bangalore.

Sharma, A., and Vekateshwarlu, D., (2007), Quality Issues in Higher Education, University News, 45(15), New Delhi.

Sharma, Bhuvanesh, (2010), *Consciousness Based Education to Incorporate Values in Higher Education*, University News, 48(39), New Delhi.

Sharma, Namrata, *et al.* (1995), Usefulness of the Computer Course for Principals and College Teachers – Views of the Participnts, Journal of Higher Education, Feb.

Shiv Kumar, V., (2009), *What Ails our Higher Education System?*, University News, 47(46), New Delhi.

Shoemaker, B., (1989), "Integrative Education: A Curriculum for the Twenty-First Century," OSSC Bulletin 33(2).

Shukla, J.J., Ambedkar, B.R., (1974), Gandhi and Tagore–A Comparative Study, Karnavati Publication, Ahmedabad.

Simha, Sasadhar (1962), Social Thinking of Rabindranath Tagore, Asia Publishing House, New Delhi.

Singh, A.K., (2007), Contextualising Higher Education in India, University News, 45(32), New Delhi.

Singh, R.P., *Moral Dilemmas in the Era of Globalisation*, University News, 48(39), New Delhi.

Sinha, S.N.P., (2002), *Towards Inculcating Value in Education*, University News, 39(48), New Delhi.

Solanki, A.B., (1958), The Teaching of Correlation in Basic Education. Navajivan Publication House, Ahmedabad.

Srivastav, A.K., and Srivastavameenu, (2005), Integrated Curriculum for Plant Sciences in the Context of UGC Regulations, 2003, Univerity News, 43(48), New Delhi.

Sudha Rao, K. and Mithilesh K. Singh, (2006), "University Education in India: Challenges Ahead", University News, Vol. (45), New Delhi.

Sundarajan, N., (2002), *Value Education: The Mission Link in Higher Education*, University News, 40(38), New Delhi.

Swamy Raju Narayana, (2010), Changing Role of Teachers in Strengthening Value Based Education, University News, 48(39), New Delhi.

Symes, C., and Mclntyre, J. (eds.) (2000), Working Knowledge; The New Vocationalism and Higher Education, Open University Press, Buckingham.

Tagore, Rabindranath, (1917), My Reminiscences, The MacMillan & Co., New York.

Tagore, Rabindranath, (1917), Personality, MacMillan & Co., London.

Tagore, Rabindranath, (1922), Creative Unity, MacMillan & Co., London.

Tagore, Rabindranath, (1929), "Ideals of Education", MacMillan & Co., London.

Tagore, Rabindranath, (1966), A Tagore Reader, edited by Amiya Chakravarthy: Beacon Press, Boston.

Tagore, Rabindranath, (1980), Our Universe: Translated by Indu Dutt, Jaico Publishing House, Bombay.

Tagore, Rabindranath, (1961), Towards Universal Man, Asia Publishing House, New York.

Talk to Khadi Vidayala Students, (1942), Sevak, 15th Feb. CW 75.

The Commonwealth of Learning, (2002), An Introduction to Open and Distance Learning available from http://www.col.org/odl intro.odl.htm

The Visvabharathi: Quarterly (April-July),73(4).

The World Bank (2000), Higher Education in Developing Countries: Peril and Promise. The Report of the Task Force on Higher Education, Washington D.C.

Tinio Victoria L., (2003), ICT in Education, can be found at http://www.eprimers.org and http://www.apdip.net.

UNESCO (1996), Learning, the Treasure within: The Report of the International Commission on Education in the Twenty-first Century. UNESCO, Paris.

UNESCO, (1998), Higher Education in the Twenty-first Century: Vision and Action, The Final Report of the World Conference on Higher Education, UNESCO, Paris.

UNESCO, (1998). Global Student Mobilisation Report, IDP, Education Australia Ltd., Sept H.E. in India, Vision and Action, Country Paper, UNESCO Conference on HE in 21st Century, Paris.

UNESCO, (2007), Higher Education in a Globalised Society, UNESCO Education Paper WTO.

Uttaryan, (2010), Vision on Education, Gandhi and Tagore: The Indian Response, New Delhi.

Vid Victor Garcia Hoz *et al.* (1995), *Personalised Education Treaty*, Ed., Rialp, Madrid.

Vijayan Nambiar K.K., (2007), Strategies of Guidance Based Education, Neelakamal Pub. Pvt. Ltd., Hyderabad.

Vyes, Nitin, J., (2010), *Spirituality, Morality, and Science as a Quest in Human Identity*, University News, 48(08), New Delhi.

Wang, F. and Hannafin M.J., (2005), Design Based Research and Technology-enhanced Learning Environment, Educational Technology Research and Development, 53(4), 5-23.

Whitehead, A.N., (1967), The Aim of Education, The Free Press, New York.

Whitehead, A.N., (1933), *Adventure of Ideas*, MacMillan & Co., New York.

Whitehead, A.N., (1929), the Aims of Education and other Essays, Macmillan, New York.

Will, George, (1994), The Leveling Wind, Penguin Books, New York.

Yash Pal Committee Recommendation, (2011), Government of India, New Delhi.

Index

D